STUCK IN
YESTERDAY

Praise for *Stuck in Yesterday*

"In this book, author Gustavo Monje seeks to present spiritual practices for wellness from his Indigenous lineages and the offerings of his teachers. These holistic traditions offer insight into what it means to live a healthy and balanced life even with the challenges that we face in today's world. His approach in writing this book is to make these practices available to everyday people, students, parents, families, and communities who can adopt and embrace new ways of being and doing in their relationships with themselves and each other. This book offers fundamental hope that we can make changes in our own lives to improve conditions for us and the natural world that sustains us."

— **Ann Filemyr, PhD, Founder & Director of the PhD in Visionary Practice and Regenerative Leadership, Southwestern College, Santa Fe, NM**

"Gustavo Monje writes about purpose and vision with the clarity of both a scholar and a sage. Drawing from the teachings of Shrii Shrii Anandamurti, a modern yogic guru, he has done the essential work of translating profound spiritual philosophy into practical tools for meaningful living. His words carry the maturity of more than twenty-five years of yogic practice, the ancestral wisdom of his Indigenous lineage, and the grounded perspective of his eighteen years as a college professor. *Stuck in Yesterday* is both a map and a companion for anyone seeking to reconnect with purpose and find holistic pathways toward balance and fulfillment."

— **Dada Vishvarupananda, Yoga Therapist, *Acharya*, and Global Director of AMURT, Rockville, MD**

"In a world full of quick fixes, especially on the psychological and spiritual levels, it is refreshing to find books like *Stuck in Yesterday*—books that don't ask us to fix ourselves, but to remember ourselves. Gustavo Monje strikes just the right balance between sharing his beliefs and the practices that have worked for him, while also opening space for his vulnerability, uncertainties, and limitations. This is the kind of posture that makes me trust a mentor, because only those who have lived and learned enough to be at ease with their own brokenness, imperfections, and doubts can humbly guide others beyond them."

— **Gustavo Prudente, Life Coach Trainer and Associate Director and Chief of Staff of Legacy Groupe in Geneva, Switzerland**

STUCK IN YESTERDAY

Visionary Practices for Building a Purposeful Future

Gustavo Monje,
PhD Candidate

Q'ENTE
BOOKS

FALLS CHURCH, VIRGINIA

Cover and interior design by Andra Monje
Content Editor: Laura June Rose

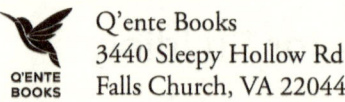

Q'ente Books
3440 Sleepy Hollow Rd
Falls Church, VA 22044

For information regarding special discounts for bulk purchases, please contact:
Q'ente Books publisher at connect@qentebooks.com.

Library of Congress Cataloging-in-Publication Data
Names: Monje, Gustavo, 1982- author.
Title: Stuck in Yesterday: Visionary Practices for Building a Purposeful Future
Description: Falls Church, Virginia : Q'ente Books, 2026 |
Includes bibliographical references and index.
Identifiers: LCCN 2025927153
Subjects: Personal Growth | Spirituality | Yoga Philosophy |
BISAC: SELF-HELP / Personal Growth / General | SELF-HELP / Spiritual |
SELF-HELP / Motivational & Inspirational.
Classification: LCC BF637 | DDC 158

ISBN: 979-8-9939495-0-5 (print)
ISBN: 979-8-9939495-1-2 (ebook)

Printed in the United States.

To my brother David,
with whom every conversation risks turning into a
comedy sketch of our favorite childhood films and to
every reader who has ever felt stuck in yesterday.

May these pages remind you that the past does
not define you and that purpose is what carries you forward.

Contents

Part Three
Your Vision Seed

Part Four
Your Principles of Success

Part Five

Your Visionary Practices

Part Six

Your Visionary Action Plan

An Initial Invitation

Some days, I try to imagine the future. I close my eyes and try to picture a life that feels clean, fresh, possible. But it's like trying to run underwater. Every step is heavy. Every thought drags me back to the mistakes I made and the chances I lost. People say, "Move on," but they don't see the walls that I see in my head.

I want to believe there's more for me. I want to believe I'm not just my biggest mistakes. But I don't know how to get there. I am trapped. Stuck. No one has a time machine to take me into the future.

FRANCESCA, A FRIEND AND FORMER STUDENT, shared these words with me when she was feeling stuck in yesterday. I assured her that she was not trapped forever. She was becoming, and there was more for her ahead. If you are here reading these words, then something inside you still believes there's more for you than your current situation. I believe that too. While this book is not a time machine, it is a lantern for the path ahead, guiding you out of yesterday's shadows and into tomorrow's light.

A Guide Into the Light of Your Future

Stuck in Yesterday: Visionary Practices for Building a Purposeful Future is written for anyone who has ever felt trapped by their past, by the

1

pain of a broken relationship, the weight of a poor decision, or the confusion of losing direction. If you've ever asked yourself—*How do I move forward when part of me is stuck?*—then this book is for you.

You may be emerging from a personal rock-bottom moment, rebuilding after incarceration, grief, divorce, or another major life disruption. Wherever you find yourself, this book meets you where you are and invites you to take your next steps toward greater purpose.

The title *Stuck in Yesterday* is inspired by Robert Zemeckis and Bob Gale's film *Back to the Future* (1985). In the film, Marty McFly is accidentally sent back in time, where he accidentally disrupts his parents' relationship, thus jeopardizing his very existence. To return to his own time, Marty must face the challenge of repairing this rupture. With the help of his mentor, Doc Brown, he begins the difficult work of mending what was broken so that he can find his way home. For many people, Marty's predicament is a metaphorical mirror of their situation: Life can leave us stuck in moments we didn't choose, held back by unresolved pain, regret, or punishment.

Thankfully, Marty wasn't alone and neither are you. We often need a guide, someone or something to help us navigate the repair. For Marty, his guide was Doc. For you, this book can play a similar role. Through this book, you have access to the wisdom my mentors have passed down to me and the ancestral knowledge I carry. Combined with your inner knowing and your ancestors, we are a team rooting for your success with deep love and compassion.

What Qualifies Me to Be Your Guide?

As we begin this journey together, I want you to know something from the start. I too have gone down roads where I lost my way or where I made a huge mess of things. I've lived with the regret of destroying important relationships. I have made mistakes from a lack of maturity or self-control. I have also witnessed firsthand people very close to me having to rebuild their lives after losing everything. So,

I'm not writing this as someone who has it all figured out. I'm writing this having been stuck in yesterday myself but also having slowly and steadily found a way forward with the strategies in this text.

This is a book about Visionary Practices: tools that help people access their inner wisdom and expand their awareness. In my Quechua-Andean lineage, a *paqo* (shaman) is a visionary practitioner, serving as a bridge between the physical and spiritual worlds. As a paqo myself, formally initiated and trained in the mountains of Peru, I have been entrusted to teach, and I have felt called to help people expand their hearts and cultivate self-love.

My recent fieldwork for my dissertation in Indigenous wellness practices has strengthened my spiritual work. These studies were conducted for my doctoral degree in Visionary Practice and Regenerative Leadership. In that program, which emphasizes spiritual intelligence as a leadership tool, I have explored how ancient traditions can help people heal, grow, and serve the modern world in meaningful ways, which is why I will present them to you in this book.

As a college professor, I help students learn professional writing and rhetorical strategy, but I also invite them engage with the knowledge of this book. Most of them are first-year college students still trying to find their way in the world. My classroom becomes a laboratory not only to improve as writers, but also as a place where they can understand themselves better and what they're here to do.

Earlier in my journey, I trained formally as a life coach and spent many years working as an emotional fitness coach. In one-on-one sessions and in the Higher Purpose retreats I organized, I sat with people during some of the most uncertain and vulnerable moments of their lives. I listened, and I reminded them of what they already carried. Everything in this book comes from experience. These are not ideas I read and passed along. They are the very practices I live by. I have used them in coaching, in ceremony, in teaching, and in my own healing. I offer them here not just because they are beautiful or inspiring but because they work.

Visionary Practices

Visionary Practices are techniques, rituals, or methods to help you see beyond the ordinary and broaden your vision, allowing you to overcome limitations. They help open your intuition and help you understand things more clearly. My first significant exposure to Visionary Practices began when I was 17 years old. I was on my way to Antioch College in Yellow Springs, OH for my college admission interview on a Greyhound bus from Washington DC. I sat next to a man who was reading. We rode all night, and it wasn't until the next morning that I spoke to him. I offered him some snacks and will never forget his response: "I can't take food right now. I haven't done my meditation yet. I am a monk." That moment sparked the beginning of my spiritual journey.

I shared things I was bringing for my interview and told him all about my plans at the time. He listened, examining me with a smile. Before we parted, he took my address and invited me to a meditation retreat in Missouri, which was far away from where I lived. I considered it politely, though most likely, I would never have gone if he hadn't surprised me with such kindness a few weeks later. One day, I received a package in the mail—a small box with a book about meditation, a CD of meditation music, and some pamphlets about the retreat in Missouri. There was also the contact information to a local teacher I could learn from. I remember feeling goosebumps, wondering who on Earth would be this thoughtful to a boy who was met in passing. Now, more than twenty years later, I thank Dada Gana, the monk on the bus, for his invitation. I completed the pilgrimage to the retreat in Missouri, not without obstacles. Yet, I was rewarded with learning my first Visionary Practice—meditation.

In some meditation practices, one uses a mantra with a deep meaning to expand the mind and merge with something greater than self. Likewise, other forms of Visionary Practices expand your heart and outlook. After learning meditation, I found the more I practiced, the more my compassion and awareness grew. However, I wouldn't call it a "Visionary Practice" until decades later.

My interview at Antioch went well, and I enrolled as a student that fall. There was a wonderful professor there named Dr. Ann Filemyr, PhD, who eventually would introduce me to the term "Visionary Practices," though not during that time. At Antioch, she was my college advisor, nurturing my academic growth. Yet, she became a spiritual mentor too, inviting me to my first sweat lodge ceremony in the tradition of her teacher Grandmother Keewaydinoquay, a beloved Anishinaabeg elder. Twenty years later, I pursued a PhD degree in the program Ann founded called Visionary Practice and Regenerative Leadership at Southwestern College in New Mexico. A new circle began—our academic and spiritual lives intertwining once again.

Ann's program invited doctoral students to explore learning through dreams, ritual, pilgrimages, art, and deep listening, not just to learn academic theories. One day, while we were visiting Petroglyph National Monument near Albuquerque, New Mexico, Ann explained Visionary Practice in the following way: "We have the capacity to expand our awareness. We have the capacity to go beyond what someone else tells us is real." Whether that happens through a dream, a piece of art, a conversation with a mentor, or meditation, Visionary Practices are about being in relationship with something greater than self.

In this book, I am offering Visionary Practices to help you find yourself, heal the past, and step into a future rooted in who you truly are. You will see the Visionary Practice icon on the previous page when it's time to engage with a new practice. This book can help you find deeper meaning regardless of where you are in your journey, or it can help rebuild your life from rock-bottom. Together, we will unlock strategies to help you know your purpose, get clear on your values, and plant a Vision Seed. You won't be asked to fix yourself. You'll be invited to remember yourself. Along the way, you'll move through six key milestones to build what I call your Higher Purpose Codex, each one designed to bring you closer to a life of greater meaning, alignment, and direction.

The Higher Purpose Codex

First, what is a codex? A codex is a collection of codes. For the Quechua shamans of the Andes Mountains, teachings are understood as codes. As part of my *Yachacha Pampa Paqo* (shaman of wisdom) training with an elder named Tupac T'ito Kuntur, I was guided through several teacher codes of philosophy and practice to assist me in my spiritual life and sharing of the lineage. This is why I have chosen to structure the teachings of this book into a codex, to pass knowledge onto you in a way that reflects my Quechua lineage and worldview.

Let me be clear. The knowledge presented in this book comes from varied sources, including my spiritual teachers. I am not asking you to adopt my cultural views or become a paqo yourself. Instead, I am offering you these teachings in the best way I know how, that is, aligned with my deepest truths, reflective of my homeland, and with your best interest in mind.

Here are the codes that you will build to create a personal manifesto of self-knowledge and action, so you can live a more purposeful life. Write your codes in a journal or a device that you can easily access to make changes and for reflection:

Code One
My Higher Purpose is...

This is where it all begins and what will guide everything that follows. You'll reflect deeply, ask the right questions, and listen inwardly until your purpose begins to speak through you. The objective is not to invent something grand or polished. Instead, it's about uncovering the truth that's already alive inside you and naming it in a way that feels honest and alive. Your purpose statement defines why you are here on this planet and what you're meant for. It defines your unique nature. I know how challenging this can sound, but there is a way to uncover this if you follow the steps in this book.

Code Two
My Core Values for interacting with others are...
My Core Values for keeping peace with myself are...

These are the guiding principles that help you move through the world with integrity. They are your personal indicators of what it means to be good. When you know what you stand for, you don't need to chase approval. These values garner respect, protect your inner peace, and anchor your choices.

Code Three
To bring my Higher Purpose to action, I will
plant the following Vision Seed(s)...

This is where purpose takes form. A Vision Seed is a purpose-driven goal or project. What is the goal, the calling, or the legacy you feel drawn to bring into the world that reflects your Higher Purpose? Your work becomes more powerful when it is mission oriented and enacted with strong moral values.

Code Four
To help my Vision Seed take root and thrive,
these are my Principles of Success...

We'll define what success truly means for you and how it can keep you resilient and focused. These principles will help you keep moving forward not just when your Vision Seed is struggling to grow, but in your overall journey. These are the principles to help you find success in your Vision Seed and also to live life well.

Code Five
To ensure my mental and spiritual expansion, I will engage with the following Visionary Practices...

As mentioned before, Visionary Practices help you stay connected to your inner wisdom and your soul's journey. They help you listen beyond the noise of daily life and tap into the deeper knowing that guides your path. Whether through meditation, reflective writing, prayer, or time in nature, these practices expand your awareness and renew your sense of purpose.

Code Six
To provide clarity and direction for my Vision Seed, I will create the following Visionary Action Plan...

Your vision will remain a dream unless you commit to real steps. A Visionary Action Plan helps you translate your insights into motion. You'll define clear steps, frameworks, and evaluative tools to grow your Vision Seed. When you have clarity and follow through, even imperfectly, the seeds you pant grow.

Writing Your Codes

By the time we reach the final pages, you'll have more than insight. You'll have a foundation—a living codex of self-knowledge you can return to whenever life feels uncertain. These codes can rebuild your life, shape your legacy, or create true alignment for all your decisions. You can always update them over time because they are living aspects of your authentic self.

Each time you write a new code, you will be reminded to review previous codes in the Higher Purpose Codex. This will enable you to see how the new code you are writing aligns with previous intentions. Draft your codes in one place in a journal, and inscribe new codes as additions in one location. You don't want to declare codes and have them remain isolated from each other. Instead, you should join each code with the others, so they can exist in alignment with one another. To review the original structure of the codex at any time, refer back to the "Initial Invitation" of this book or see the final chapter: Final Weavings and Invitations.

The Knowledge Keepers of this Book

As I described earlier, this knowledge didn't come from me alone. The insights and practices you'll encounter here were shaped by extraordinary teachers, who showed me a light when I was in darkness. They are the mentors and guides who have helped me and can help you feel free if you are feeling stuck. I've collected many of their best teachings and packaged them for you right here in this text.

Much of the knowledge stems from the teachings of my guru Shrii Shrii Anandamurti, whom I refer to throughout this book simply as Baba. I chose to name him informally to give the reader the impression that Baba is like an friend or grandfather, full of great stories and easy to relate to. To me, and to many around the world, Baba was more than a yoga guru. He was a treasure of practical wisdom too. His teachings on what it means to be human, consciousness, ethical values, and secrets of success form many of the core principles of this book's framework. I never met Baba in person because he left his body long before I learned about him. Instead, I saw him in dreams and was lucky to be transformed by his books and the students he left behind.

You may be wondering whether you signed up to learn yoga philosophy by reading this book and whether you really want to. I assure you that although many of the teachings in this book come from the world of yoga, they can still offer you practical knowledge and a fresh perspective in times of adversity. Also, as I mentioned before, this book is not intended to convert you to a different religion, make you a yogi, or have you follow any of my teachers. I am only giving credit where credit is due and synthesizing knowledge that I think can be most beneficial to you.

Baba is not the only teacher whose presence lives in these pages. I have already briefly introduced you to Ann Filemyr, my spiritual and PhD mentor, and Tupac, my lineage elder. You'll meet more of them in the pages to come, who challenged me and believed in me when I forgot how to believe in myself. They have shaped my spiritual life and helped me live in the real world too. You may feel the presence of my teachers as you read, reassuring you that you're not walking this path alone. Because you're not.

I don't claim to have all the answers. But I've walked this path, learning as much as I could from my mistakes and from my mentors, and I've walked it with others like you. Here, I offer lived experience, ancient knowledge, and a heartfelt commitment to your growth. Wherever you are on your path, whether you're just awakening to the idea of purpose, or returning to it after a long detour, I wish you clarity, strength, and deep self-trust. May this book be your Doc Brown as you step into your future with renewed purpose and vision. You are not stuck forever. You are becoming. Don't put the book down yet. Let's start the journey of repair now.

Part One

Your Higher Purpose

Find the Ruby in Your Heart

IF YOU HAVE EVER gone through a traumatic experience, you may have felt like giving up hope. Yet, if you are here, you have not. Perhaps you asked yourself: *What is still shining within me? What part of my humanity can I hold on to?* If so, you have begun to look for your Higher Purpose—the "ruby in your heart"—as my mentor Ann Filemyr would say.

Viktor Frankl: The Power of Higher Purpose

Viktor Frankl was in his thirties, a young professional full of promise and ambition, trying to make a name for himself in the world of psychiatry during the 1940s in Austria.[1] He worked hard to be a good son, a good student, and above all, a good person. He believed in living a life of integrity and dedication, and he was eager to build a future that balanced his promising career with the joys of family life.

Marrying Tilly Grosser felt like the first step in achieving that dream. She was a strong match for Viktor—kindhearted, steady, and compassionate. A nurse at Rothschild Hospital, Tilly dedicated her days to the care of others. Like Viktor, she had high hopes for the simple joys of a typical life. She wanted to be a mother one day, to fill her home with the laughter of her family. But the world outside their doorstep had other plans for Jewish families like theirs. As the Nazis tightened their grip on Europe, everything Viktor and Tilly had hoped for began to crumble in their hands. The first devastating blow came when the Nazis ordered the newlywed couple to abort their first child nine months after they were married. The loss was heartbreaking, a cruel reminder that their lives were no longer their own.

In September of 1942, Viktor and Tilly were arrested and deported to the Terezin Ghetto in what is today the Czech Republic, along with his mother and father. Meanwhile, Viktor's brother Walter and his wife attempted to flee to other parts of Europe. In the purgatory of the Terezin Ghetto, the cruelty of the Nazis hovered over their shoulders at every moment. Six months later, came the breaking point—Viktor's father died of exhaustion, eliminating whatever hope was left for keeping the family together.

A year and a half later, Viktor, Tilly, and his mother were transported to Auschwitz-Birkenau, one of World War II's most notorious death camps. There, his 65-year-old mother was separated from him and murdered in the gas chambers. Tilly was forced to go to another camp, leaving Viktor completely stripped of the life he knew. Each day, he wrestled with the uncertainty of the future. Each day he felt like he was stuck in the past, questioning whether life still held meaning after so much had been taken from him.

While imprisoned, Viktor began comforting new arrival detainees, all the while feeling the anxiety of not knowing the fate of his wife and the rest of his family members. After the Allied Forces liberated the camps in 1945, desperate to learn of his wife's fate, he made the long journey back to Austria. But the news that awaited him was unbearable. Tilly, his young bride, had died in Bergen-Belsen camp. His brother Walter and his wife were also captured and murdered in Auschwitz. In just a few days, Viktor came to discover that everyone he had loved had been murdered by the Nazis.

Viktor stood in the wreckage of his life. He was a man who had followed all the rules only to have everything ripped away. And yet, in the depths of his grief, something within him still flickered. He couldn't change what had happened, couldn't undo the losses. Yet, he dared to ask: *What now? What meaning could I find in this pain? What purpose could I bring to the world, even after all of this?*

Amid that terrible suffering, Viktor discovered something extraordinary. Within himself, he stood firm and said, *No* to the names the Nazis called him. *No* to the treatment that tried to crush his spirit. *No* to the notion that their brutality could erase his value. Instead, he clung to an unyielding truth: I have something to offer. I am a human being. I have value. I have a purpose beyond this suffering, beyond what they call me, beyond the way they treat me.

This wasn't a denial of his circumstances. Viktor didn't ignore the pain or pretend the horrors weren't real. He fully lived those experiences, felt the torment of them in every moment. However, he also knew that another understanding existed deep inside him, a part untouched by suffering and undefined by cruelty. That inner knowing was his purpose, a compass pointing to something greater than his suffering.

Viktor's renewed understanding of his Higher Purpose became a mission: to help others find theirs, especially in suffering. After surviving the Holocaust and losing his entire family, he poured his grief into rebuilding a life of service. With the support of friends, he rewrote his lost manuscript and became the director of the Vienna Neurological Policlinic. His book *Man's Search for Meaning* (1946), written in just nine days, quickly became a postwar bestseller and a guiding light for those facing despair.

Recognized by his peers as the "third Viennese school of psychotherapy," Frankl's work earned international acclaim. He went on to teach at Harvard and other global institutions, always emphasizing personal responsibility, inner freedom, and the human capacity to choose meaning, even in life's darkest moments.

Understanding one's inner compass or Higher Purpose offers tremendous benefit: the ability to expand beyond the labels, the circumstances, and even the pain that surrounds you. The challenge is to face what is happening in the outer world and hold on to what shines within you, no matter how challenging the outer world appears.

You may or may not have ever experienced as great a tragedy as Viktor Frankl. Still, I have no doubt that your challenges test your limits. If someone calls you unworthy or if someone labels you a failure, you may feel like giving up, becoming the labels people impose on you. Yet, by knowing your Higher Purpose, like Frankl, you find a way to overcome these labels and self-doubts. You find a way to remain your true self.

Why Do Ordinary People Lose Touch with Their Sense of Purpose?

This is a question I've explored in depth with Gustavo Prudente, my coaching teacher. A gifted coach and mentor from Sao Paulo, Brazil, Gustavo has trained life coaches and guided countless individuals through the process of discovering and reconnecting with their life's purpose. According to Gustavo, the biggest issue for people who feel disconnected from their purpose is dissociation.

Dissociation occurs when there is a gap between what we truly feel and what we have been conditioned to believe is acceptable. Imagine a child who experiences something unfair. The child feels the injustice and the anger that comes with it. But then, an adult tells them: "No, this is normal. You shouldn't be angry." What happens then? The child learns not to trust their feelings. They learn to dissociate. Over time, they learn to discard their intuition.

Gustavo explained to me that on a rational level, the child accepts the adult's version of reality. They think: *Okay, what's happening to me is good for me, and I am not angry.* But in their body, they still feel that it is wrong, and emotionally they remain angry. That disconnection between experience and expression, between feeling and knowing, is the seed of dissociation. Chronic dissociation causes people to feel lost, to not know who they are or where they're going. When we are disconnected from our purpose, we often seek secondary ways to soothe our emptiness. This can happen through distractions, external validation, or even self-destructive habits. However, true fulfillment only comes from healing disconnections within ourselves.

This entire book—your Higher Purpose statement, the exercises, your Vision Seed—is actually a process of reintegration, as Gustavo taught me. It is about bringing language into alignment with deep physical, emotional, and spiritual knowing. When your words and actions match your deeper truth, you feel connected. And when you feel connected, you know where you are meant to be. By identifying your Higher Purpose, you are not just filling in an aspect of your personality. You are reclaiming a connection to something essential, something that you have always had but may have lost.

Idea and Ideology

In the summer of 1959, Baba, who I mentioned previously, gave a series of powerful talks to a small group of his followers in his hometown of Jamalpur, India. That same year, his followers transcribed these talks, which were delivered in a mix of English and Hindi, into a book called *Idea and Ideology*.[2] The book covered many topics, including some of Baba's most important ideas about philosophy, politics, and economics. The title *Idea and Ideology* has always stood out to me. It reflects the difference between a simple idea and the actions needed to bring that idea to life. Borrowing this title as an analogy, we can explore how understanding and living in alignment with a Higher Purpose transforms a mere idea into a guiding principle, shaping your values and actions.

At its core, an idea is a thought—a concept born in the mind, emerging from consciousness. But not all ideas are created equal.

Some are fleeting, tied to passing whims or immediate needs. Others are transformative, carrying the weight of meaning and the potential to shape your life. Among these, your Higher Purpose stands out as one of the most subtle and elevated ideas you can have about yourself. Your Higher Purpose is an idea that transcends the everyday and taps into the essence of who you are. It invites you to look beyond the roles you play or the circumstances you face and ask profound questions: *Who am I? Why am I here?* These ideas, are not limited by the constraints of the material world. Instead, they are an expansive reflection of your unique capacity to contribute to the greater whole.

When you become aware of your Higher Purpose, it's as though you're handed a map. Suddenly, you have a clear direction for how to navigate your journey. From this awareness, you develop an ideology, a framework for living your life in alignment with your purpose.

Figure 1
From Idea to Ideology

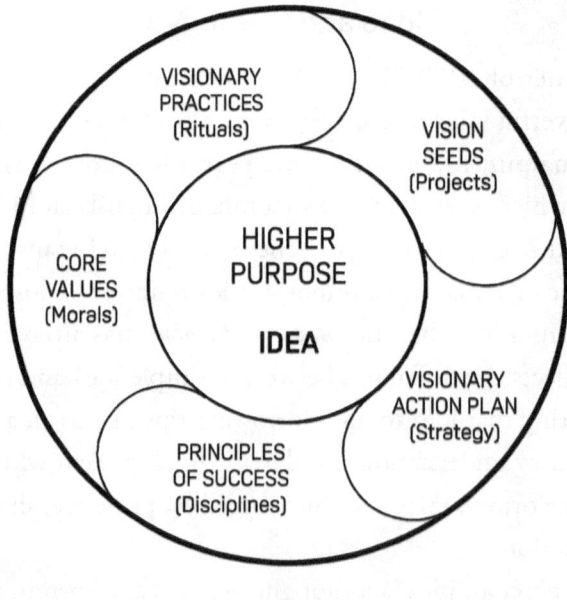

IDEOLOGY

Figure one shows how your Higher Purpose, as an idea, can be developed into a personal ideology built from the elements in the Higher Purpose Codex. In this way, your purpose creates a foundation for every decision you make.

The true power of your Higher Purpose lies in its ability to inspire action. It serves as a launching pad, propelling you toward choices and behaviors that align with your deepest values and aspirations. For instance, if your Higher Purpose is to foster connection, that idea might inspire you to nurture relationships, build community, or simply approach others with kindness and understanding. The idea becomes the source of your actions and grounds your actions in meaning and intention. However, it's important to recognize that your Higher Purpose is not something fixed or final. Some traditional approaches to coaching or life planning present purpose as a rigid statement, something you define once and then implement for the rest of your life. You shouldn't treat purpose as a static plan. It's a living, breathing understanding of yourself that evolves as you do.

At one stage of life, you may craft a purpose statement that brings clarity and enthusiasm. You live by that statement, explore its depth, and embody its meaning. Then, at some point, you may reach a plateau and begin to question: *Is this still my purpose?* When this happens, it doesn't mean your purpose was wrong. It simply means that you have grown. Rather than discard your purpose, it is a time to revisit it, reflect on how it has shaped your journey, and refine it to better align with your current understanding of yourself. Sometimes, your Higher Purpose statement itself changes as you gain new insights. Other times, the words remain the same, but their meaning deepens.

Four Levels of Awareness

In *Idea and Ideology (1959)*, Baba introduced a profound way to understand the human experience through four levels of awareness:

- *Chitta:* the Survival, or the "Fight-or-Flight" State
- *Aham:* the Ego, or "The Doer" State
- *Mahat:* the Witnessing State
- *Atman:* the Infinite Soul State

These Sanskrit concepts describe how the mind operates at different levels of awareness, shaping the way we perceive life and our goals. While Baba originally presented these as "chambers of the mind," I am reframing them here as states of being or levels of awareness that can influence how you understand your Higher Purpose. These levels of awareness also reflect an evolutionary journey: how human beings have progressed over time in the way they think, feel, and relate to the world. Let's explore each level, both in terms of its role in our evolution and its influence on our present-day choices.

Chitta

The reactive Chitta (CHIT-tah) state is instinct-driven and rooted in the primal need for safety and security. According to Baba, the Chitta is not a self-aware state. It is simply a mental screen—a stage where thoughts, threats, emotions, and instincts appear and disappear. A helpful comparison for the Chitta is a radio constantly scanning through stations, picking up whatever signal is strongest at the moment. Just as the radio itself does not choose what to play, the Survival State simply receives and reacts to whatever is happening in the environment.

According to Baba, tens of thousands of years ago, the early human mind primarily operated in the Survival State—constantly focused on finding food, avoiding predators, and reproducing. This state of mind developed to keep us alive in dangerous environments. Yet, even today, it remains active within us. When we operate from the Survival State, our thoughts are scattered, shallow, and may be dominated by fear or anxiety. A Higher Purpose statement crafted at this level of the mind may be:

My Higher Purpose is to survive.

However, more accurately, because the Chitta lacks reflective capacity and long-term vision, it is not likely that a Higher Purpose statement can even be formed at this level. Goals formed at this level of awareness tend to focus on immediate needs or quick solutions like staying safe, avoiding risk, or seeking temporary comfort.

Aham

As humans evolved beyond the survival state, they developed a deeper sense of self-awareness, giving rise to the Ego—"The Doer" State, or Aham *(AH-hum)*. This is the level where we recognize ourselves as in-dividuals, distinct from others. With this awareness came the ability to reason, create, act, and plan for the future, but also the development of vanity and domination. In "the Doer" State, we focus on action and achievement. For example, early humans began creating tools, forming social structures, and striving for influence within their com-munities. This led to desires for excelling at work, earning recognition, or pursuing material success. While "the Doer" State helps us build individuality, intellect, and accomplishments, it can also cause one to be driven by material pursuits.

Gustavo Prudente, my coach, warns that much of the modern self-help and coaching industry operates at the level of "the Doer" or Ego State in ways that can be harmful. Some programs promise a perfect life, urging people to "manifest" success or choose joy over suf-fering at all times. While positive thinking has its place, this mindset can easily slip into toxic positivity, the unrealistic expectation that we should always be thriving, always happy, always at our peak. Anyone who has raised children knows that life doesn't work that way. Gus-tavo says one of the greatest lessons of parenthood is reconciling with ambivalence, the idea that joy and sorrow can exist simultaneously.

Ambivalence is not about feeling happy one day and sad the next. Rather, it is about experiencing both at the same time. For example, a parent might feel tremendous love and pride as they watch their child take their first bus ride to school, while simultaneously grieving the loss of their little one's dependence on them. Or they may feel deep gratitude for the time spent caring for their child while also feeling exhausted, frustrated, or even longing for personal freedom. These emotions don't cancel each other out. They coexist, shaping the parent's experience in a way that is both beautiful and challenging. Holding space for ambivalence is essential to developing personal self-care tools.

All too often, people get overwhelmed by their own Ego or "Doer" State. Instead of finding balance, they over-identify with the limited range of emotions in the Aham. They become completely immersed in the highs and lows of their feelings and actions, creating over-dramatic personalities that can be exhausting for themselves and others. A Higher Purpose statement written at the Aham level may sound like:

> *My Higher Purpose is to become the best in my field,*
> *so I can make a name for myself and be remembered.*

It may be shallow and focus only on something you want to accomplish in the short-term. Goals at this level tend to focus on action, titles, acquisition, and fame.

Mahat

The next step in human evolution was the expansion of the Witnessing State, or Mahat (MAH-hut), where human awareness moves beyond ego-driven desires to a deeper sense of contemplation and connection. While ego plays a practical role in the fulfillment of your Higher Purpose and Vision Seed because they both require some kind of action to be implemented, the Witnessing State reflects a more peaceful and expansive state of mind, where we can observe life without being consumed by it.

Imagine walking in nature. At first, your mind might race with to-do lists and worries. But as you keep walking, you start to notice the surrounding beauty. The noise of daily life fades, and you feel calm and present. In the calmness of nature, you go into the Witnessing State, where you feel light and balanced. Through the Witnessing State, we operate in a way that feels closer to the natural world.

The Mahat represents the consciousness within you that observes your shifting moods and thoughts. Baba describes the Mahat as the observer, the bridge between the Aham (the Ego) and the Atman (Infinite soul). When we enter the Witnessing State, we understand that we can separate ourselves from our negative emotions and rather than react to them, observe them. In the mindful thinking of the Witnessing State, we recognize interconnection and can see how past experiences have shaped who we are. Further, the Witnessing State allows us to let go of the need to control everything. We begin to accept that on some days we will feel amazing, and on other days we will feel terrible, or even that some days we will feel both amazing and terrible. We accept this because, in the Witnessing state, we can look at these cycles of emotions more objectively. From the level of the Mahat, we may craft a purpose statement that sounds like:

My Higher Purpose is to live in the present moment
and respond to life with compassion, grace, and integrity.

Goals made at this level are detached from vain pursuits and may seek inner rewards like peace or wisdom.

Atman

At the deepest level of awareness is the Infinite Soul State, or Atman (AHT-mahn), where we transcend individuality altogether and connect with the vast universe. This level reflects the ultimate stage of evolution: realizing that we are not separate beings but part of a greater, infinite consciousness.

Throughout history, spiritual seekers and mystics have described this state as one of profound unity and timelessness. It's the awareness that goes beyond thought, beyond ego, and even beyond the peaceful Witnessing State. When we operate from the Infinite Soul State, our purpose is guided by universal love, oneness, and cosmic wisdom. As Baba explains, the Atman is beyond individual consciousness itself. It is the soul experience of all beings, our most powerful and deeply connected state.

If existence were a volume knob, the Atman would be the volume at full blast—highest existence. Another word to describe this is Ananda or pure bliss. Ananda in Sanskrit is the deep, unshakable joy that tells us: *I am connected to all.* But this doesn't mean we can live every moment in the Atman, while navigating everyday life. Instead, we can strive toward attaining glimpses of the Atman State in a moment of deep meditation or ceremonial bliss. Through our temporary experiences in the Infinite Soul State, we get glimpses of our potential and our Higher Purpose. A purpose statement at the Atman level might sound like:

*My Higher Purpose is to embody the oneness of all things
and allow universal wisdom to move through me.*

Goals formed here are not bound by time or personal desire. They reflect a deeper alignment with the collective good and the oneness of everything in the cosmos.

Uncovering your Higher Purpose

Ideally, to uncover your Higher Purpose you need to be operating at the highest level of awareness possible. That doesn't mean you have to be a guru to get it. See how the following scenario illustrates moving through the Levels of Awareness, one at a time, as if peeling back the layers of your own mind:

After days immersed in the Ego State, working, and in the Survival State, navigating the hardships of everyday life, one day you go into nature to quiet the noise of the world and reconnect with yourself. By the tranquility of a waterfall, you sit quietly and close your eyes. Your breath deepens. The chatter within your mind fades as you focus more and more on your breathing. Slowly, you slip into the Witnessing State. Here, your awareness expands. You become less preoccupied with your worries. You observe your emotions without needing to fix or explain them. Peace arises, even joy.

For a moment, the waterfall puts you in a trance. You marvel at the endless streams pouring effortlessly. The sheer mystery and power of the falls reminds you of the Universe's greatness. It feels like Ananda, pure bliss. As your stillness deepens, so does your awareness. You observe clearly not only your own consciousness but the pulse of the Universe itself. You are observing something timeless. Without realizing it, you experience the Atman, the Infinite Soul State. You become barely aware of it. You hear a word, a phrase, or a feeling that lands deep within you—something that feels true. An understanding of your Higher Purpose emerges, not as a goal, but as a truth that has been there all along.

Later, as you return to everyday life, you gently re-enter "the Doer" State with renewed clarity. Sure, you are ready to jump back into your projects, but now your heart has a little more room for kindness to yourself and to all.

The key Level of Awareness to employ when uncovering your Higher Purpose is the Witnessing State. It can serve as a bridge between the wisdom of the soul and the actions of the ego. This is the same process used in art, Tarot, dream interpretation, and other intuitive practices: we take something beyond language and translate it into something concrete.

More than likely, your Higher Purpose involves the realm of the Ego because it is something you can articulate and put into action, but also, it is infused with the unknown, with the joy and guidance of the Infinite Soul State. Your Higher Purpose is the link or midpoint between these realms that allows your soul's calling to take form in the world.

Visionary Practice: Holding Space for Your Higher Purpose

This week, take a moment to set a clear intention: express to the Universe that you are ready to build your Higher Purpose Codex and ask that your Higher Purpose Statement be revealed to you in the right time.

As you move through the next chapters, you'll be guided through visionary steps to help uncover your purpose, but for now, simply open the door. Invite this deeper knowing into your life, and ask for support so that, when it arrives, your heart is ready to receive it.

You might call upon your ancestors, Christ if you are Christian, or any form of the Divine that holds meaning for you. If you feel called, visit a sacred place like a mountain, a forest, or a river, and ask the Spirit of that place to assist you. However you choose to do it, let this be an intimate ritual. Trust your intuition. Honor it with sincerity. Let your intention become a prayer or a promise to yourself. The path to your purpose begins with a willing heart and a sacred invitation.

What Being Human Reveals
About Your Purpose

IN THE 1983 FILM *MONTY PYTHON'S THE MEANING OF LIFE*, written by the Monty Python Troupe, a character opens an envelope and unveils for all of time what the meaning of life really is:

> Well, it's nothing very special...
> Try and be nice to people, avoid eating fat, read a good book every now and then, get some walking in, and try to live together in peace and harmony with people of all creeds and nations.

This answer is charming, and it might even offer some inspiration for your Core Values. But let's take a deeper look at meaning and purpose. Before exploring your individual Higher Purpose, it's worthwhile to pause and ask a broader question: What is the Higher Purpose of humanity?

By looking at the broad scope of what it means to be human, you may broaden your own understanding of your unique purpose. Across time, different cultures and philosophers have offered their own interpretations of what makes human beings unique compared to other living beings, and they have suggested many answers. In Yoga philosophy, the Sanskrit term *Dharma* beautifully captures this inquiry. For Baba, Dharma represented the inherent nature of something, its true essence and purpose. He explained, the Dharma of fire is to burn and the Dharma of water is to flow and be wet. In the same way, humanity has its own Dharma, certain natural qualities that define what it means to be human.

First, let's talk about the physical characteristics of a human being. On a physical level, we all share basic needs such as eating, sleeping, and procreating, which ensure the survival of our species. According to Baba, these characteristics are a fundamental part of what it means to be human. However, he also notes that humanity is not defined by physical characteristics alone. There are subtle qualities that go beyond the physical and instinctual. Baba described these mental and behavioral characteristics as the stages of human Dharma:[1]

- *Vistara*: the expansion of mind
- *Rasa*: flow and the ability to adapt
- *Seva*: selfless service

In this chapter, we'll explore each of these stages in depth and see how they can help you reflect on both your individual journey and the collective human experience. We will also explore a few sample purpose statements, each one focused on one of the stages of Dharma.

Vistara: The Expansion of Mind

Vistara is the inherent capacity of the mind to expand itself. As human beings, we are naturally wired to learn, grow, and evolve. From the moment we are born, we begin exploring the world around us. Whether as toddlers crawling away from our mothers to explore our home or high school graduates seeking higher levels of education, we strive to expand our place and intellect. We seek to discover new ideas and push the boundaries of science, art, and technology. We also seek to expand our influence and resources—whether it's growing our net worth, building larger networks of connections, or exploring new physical and intellectual territories. Even on a spiritual level, humans possess a unique ability to contemplate the Infinite, to envision Divinity far beyond what the senses can perceive.

Neuroplasticity, the brain's remarkable ability to gain new knowledge by forming new neural connections, is a scientific reflection of the mind's capacity to expand. Scientists have discovered humans have a natural flexibility that allows us to adapt, grow, and recover, whether we're learning new skills, navigating change, or overcoming challenges like trauma.[2] This reminds us that we are often capable of starting something new, even when we doubt our own capacity to do so. No matter how inexperienced we may be, the brain is capable of learning, provided we nurture it through consistent effort and intention.

A Case Study in Vistara

Arnold Schwarzenegger's journey is almost a perfect example of Vistara. Born in 1947 in the small Austrian village of Thal, Arnold grew up in a modest home with no running water or electricity. His father was a strict local policeman, and life in Thal was simple and predictable. Yet, even as a young boy, Arnold dreamed of something bigger. Arnold's first glimpse of a larger world came through magazines and movies. He was captivated by images of bodybuilders, some of whom would go on to star in Hollywood films. For Arnold, these images sparked a vision of what his life could be, one that expanded far beyond the confines of his rural upbringing.

At the age of 15, Arnold began to expand his body by weightlifting. The local gym in Graz, the nearest city, became his second home. He poured himself into training, visualizing himself competing on the world stage. At 18, Arnold joined the Austrian army but never forgot his dreams. During his military service, he famously went AWOL to compete in the Junior Mr. Europe Bodybuilding Competition. He won first place, solidifying his ambition to become the world's greatest bodybuilder. Arnold then moved to Munich to train professionally. His hard work paid off when he won the Mr. Universe title at just 20 years old, the youngest person ever to achieve this honor.

Arnold's vision continued to expand. He set his sights on the United States, the birthplace of the modern bodybuilding movement. In 1968, with little money and a limited grasp of English, he moved to California, where he would dominate the bodybuilding world, winning the prestigious Mr. Olympia title seven times and becoming a global icon in the sport. Imagine accomplishing all of this before becoming a Hollywood giant! While many doubted his ability to transition into acting due to his thick Austrian accent and muscular build (unusual qualities for leading male actors at the time), he defied expectations, becoming one of Hollywood's biggest action stars.

Still, he wasn't done. In 2003, he entered politics, ran for governor of California, and won, serving two terms and focusing on environmental reform and infrastructure. Arnold's life is a masterclass in mental and physical expansion. From bodybuilding to Hollywood stardom and then to holding political office, he stretched the limits of body, mind, and ambition, proving just how much a single human being can grow.

You too possess an ever-expanding capacity to learn and create. Embrace what Dr. Carol S. Dweck (2006) calls the "growth mindset," where you are more concerned with learning than being flawless. Even when you don't meet your physical goals, your mind gains experience and fortitude for the next attempt. Here is an example of a Higher Purpose statement focused on Vistara:

My Higher Purpose is to continually expand my mind, heart, and soul by embracing growth, choosing love, and increasing my faith in the lord. I am here to learn, to evolve, and to use what I discover to inspire others to move beyond their limitations.

Vistara can remind you that part of living fully is embracing your ability to stretch beyond what you thought was possible.

Rasa: Flow and the Human Ability to Adapt

Rasa, or adaptability, is the ability to adjust to life's unpredictable flow, navigating its changes with resilience and grace. Everyone knows, life does not always go as planned. Unexpected challenges, disruptions, and limitations are inevitable, and it's in these moments that our capacity for Rasa becomes essential. Adaptability is a fundamental quality of being human, enabling us to thrive even when circumstances don't align with our desires. Without adaptability, our desire to expand can lead to frustration and stagnation when obstacles arise. With adaptability, we remain flexible, open to change, and capable of aligning with life's greater flow.

Adaptability has always been a hallmark of humanity, allowing human beings not only to survive but to thrive. Across history, people have continuously demonstrated this quality in response to both external challenges and internal changes. For example, Indigenous communities like the Inuit in the Arctic and the Bedouins in the desert have survived for generations in some of the harshest environments. Through ingenuity and deep ecological knowledge, they developed clothing, tools, and social systems finely tuned to their surroundings, demonstrating human resilience in the face of extreme conditions.

For better or worse, societies have navigated (and continue to navigate) enormous transitions, such as the Industrial Revolution, which redefined how we worked and lived. Another example is the rapid acceleration into the Digital Age, which is again redefining how we work and live. The widespread use of smartphones are prime examples of how quickly we can adapt to groundbreaking innovations. Whether in terms of survival or modern innovation, the ability to flow with life's currents is a testament to our capacity for adaptability.

Flowing with the Universe's Plan

From a spiritual perspective, Rasa is the practice of aligning ourselves with the will of a higher power or cosmic flow. Embracing Rasa, we soften the grip of the ego and find peace in the understanding that life unfolds according to a larger, divine rhythm. True happiness arises not from forcing reality to meet our expectations but from discovering alignment with life as it is, trusting that even setbacks and disappointments are part of a greater plan. This trust allows us to experience life with ease and joy, even in the face of uncertainty.

Even death, which we often fear as the ultimate end, is part of the cosmic flow. For many spiritual and religious people, death is not the end of life. It is simply a transition, a merging back into the greater whole. The soul flows, continuing beyond the physical body. In this way, *Rasa* is not just about day-to-day resilience but about embracing the eternal flow of existence itself.

Resilience During the Pandemic

You remember the moment it all changed? One day, life was moving along normally with commutes, school drop-offs, crowded events, and casual handshakes. Then, everything came to a halt. The news of a global pandemic swept in like a tsunami, and in what felt like an instant, your world shifted. You found yourself navigating unfamiliar territory: logging into online classes, clocking into work and realizing some of your closest co-workers had been laid off, or waiting in long lines outside the grocery store or pharmacy. The routines you once relied on vanished, replaced by a strange new normal that you hadn't planned for at all. Still, you adapted.

You learned how to celebrate birthdays over video calls and how to find small joys while mostly staying home. You adjusted to masks and social distancing. You watched as scientists and healthcare workers around the world raced to respond, developing vaccines in record time and reshaping the boundaries of what was thought possible. Even amid grief, disruption, and fear, you noticed resilience—perhaps even your own. You made it through a time no one had prepared you for. That was *Rasa* in motion.

Both Vistara and Rasa suggest you are wired with the ability to grow and adjust. This could be a vital outlook when you encounter challenges or disappointments in your Core Values or Vision Seeds. A higher purpose statement with a focus on Rasa may sound like this:

> *My Higher Purpose is to live in harmony with the flow*
> *of life, meeting change with openness and resilience.*
> *I am here to grow through what unfolds.*

A Higher Purpose built with Rasa acknowledges that obstacles are inevitable and provides you with the flexibility to pivot, adapt, or find new ways to honor what truly matters to you.

Seva: Selfless Service

While Rasa helps us navigate life with flexibility and openness, *Seva* encourages us to serve, to the best of our capacity. What does selfless service mean? In everyday life, the word "service" is often tied to business transactions. We hear banks promote slogans like, "Serving our community since 1925," but the truth is they've been conducting financial transactions for profit. That's not true service; it's business. Seva, on the other hand, is about giving without expecting anything in return. Selfless service comes from a deep place within us, a place that seeks connection, compassion, and contribution simply because it feels right.

This natural inclination to help shows that selfless service is ingrained in who we are. Although social media can show banal and cringe-worthy sides of humanity, positive moments can also be captured beautifully. Sometimes we see people on our social media feeds caught in moments of spontaneous kindness. Videos go viral of dads rescuing their kids with swift grace, strangers saving animals trapped in danger, or someone stepping up to help an elderly person cross a busy street. What makes these moments so interesting is their authenticity. The people in these videos aren't seeking recognition. They're simply acting on instinct.

In other words, when a stranger leaps into action to save a life, they're responding to something deeply human. These actions remind us that while society often prioritizes competition, our deeper instinct is one of cooperation and care. But Seva does not have to be heroic. Even the simple act of listening to someone in need can be an act of Seva. Offering your full attention to someone who feels unheard can have a profound impact, reminding them that they matter and that they're not alone.

Doing Good Feels Good

There's a reason helping others feels good. It's even backed by science. Acts of kindness trigger the release of endorphins, the body's natural painkillers, as well as oxytocin, sometimes referred to as the "love hormone." Endorphins create a sense of euphoria, while oxytocin fosters feelings of bonding and connection. Together, these chemicals generate what psychologists call the "helper's high."[3]

Research suggests that kindness activates the brain's reward system, particularly regions linked to pleasure and satisfaction. A study conducted by the National Institutes of Health found that people who donated to charity experienced heightened activity in the brain's mesolimbic reward system, the same area that is activated by pleasurable activities like eating or listening to music.[4] Additionally, oxytocin, which is released in the brain during acts of kindness, reduces stress and promotes emotional well-being. According to research from Claremont Graduate University, elevated oxytocin levels correlate with increased generosity, further reinforcing the cycle of giving.[5] In essence, when you help others, you're not just benefiting them. You are also nurturing your own emotional and physical health.

Rabindranath Tagore, the famous Indian poet, was quoted in a United Nations' address to have said, "'I slept and dreamt that life was joy. I awoke and saw that life was service. I acted and, behold, service was joy.'"[6] His words capture a universal truth: the act of giving brings with it a profound sense of fulfillment.

Serving with Respect and According to Your Capacity

One of the most meaningful ways I practiced *Seva* was by hosting free online collective meditation gatherings every week for three years, creating a spiritual community called Vistara Circle. During one of these live streams, our discussion topic was *Seva*.

At one point, a participant typed into the chat: "What if the person you live with won't let you serve them?" I could feel the pain behind the question, perhaps the frustration of watching someone they loved struggle while feeling powerless to help. I told the group, "Sometimes, the most loving service we can offer is respect. Respecting someone enough to let them walk their own path, even when it's painful to watch, is also service."

Later, the woman who asked the question emailed me. She was a mother, heartbroken over her son's destructive behavior. She had tried everything: sending him to rehab, offering support, even covering up his mistakes. Nothing helped. I shared something I've learned through my own experience: you can offer love and support, but you cannot carry someone else's transformation. Sacrificing for others is appropriate when it comes to offering service. However, if helping others destroys you, it's no longer healthy. It may be co-dependency. The mother admitted that in her efforts to save her son, she had been losing herself.

I encouraged her to seek support, whether through therapy, a support group, or close friends who could help her navigate this difficult time. Seva is not about losing yourself in another person's struggle. It's about offering what you can, from a place of clarity, compassion, and sustainability. Seva means to give what you can, without attachment to outcome, and to work within your capacity and not over-extend yourself. Here is an example of a higher purpose focused on Seva:

> *My Higher Purpose is to be of service to others with compassion and integrity to the best of my capacity. Through presence, listening, and action, I strive to contribute to the greater whole.*

Consider how infusing aspects of Seva in your Higher Purpose statement would ensure that your goals are not only meaningful to you but genuinely helpful to the world around you.

Crafting Your Higher Purpose Statement

Now that you've explored three aspects of Dharma: the capacity to expand (Vistara), to adapt (Rasa), and to serve (Seva), you've seen part of what makes us uniquely human. But here's the beautiful truth— there's also space for your unique Dharma or purpose to be known.

Your Higher Purpose may build on the stages of Dharma, or it may stretch beyond them in unexpected ways. Perhaps you're drawn more to spiritual development, artistic expression, or intellectual discovery. Maybe you feel called to service, but not in the ways we have named. You might be here to care for animals, restore ecosystems, or uplift marginalized communities. Your purpose is not a fixed formula. It's a living expression of what makes you shine. And while it may draw from the shared beauty of being human, it will always carry your unique voice, your medicine, and your way of contributing to a more meaningful world.

Hopefully, the previous examples of purpose statements gave you a picture of the expansive scope your Higher Purpose statement could have. What's important to remember is that crafting your purpose statement should not be purely an intellectual exercise. It's an intuitive journey inward, designed to help you uncover your most authentic self. To guide you toward this experience of alignment, in the next chapter, you will work through three Visionary Practices taught to me by my mentor, Gustavo Prudente. I trust that what you uncover will reflect the very best of who you are and who you are becoming.

Weaving Together Code One
Revealing Who You Really Are

Higher purpose is not something you force into existence. It is not created by simply writing a statement or defining a goal. Instead, it emerges naturally, much like love. You don't first say, 'I love you,' and by saying it, create love. Love grows within you; you feel it. At some point, you say the words 'I love you' as a way of naming an experience that already exists.

—*Gustavo Prudente, Life Coach Trainer*

DISCOVERING YOUR HIGHER PURPOSE works the same way. In this chapter, you will work through three Visionary Practices designed to help you craft a Higher Purpose statement. I call them the three Visionary Practices that reveal who you really are:

1. Remembering your story of joy
2. Imagining your ideal day
3. Who am I? Meditation

Each of these exercises are designed to bring you into the deeper layers of your heart, where your most authentic self resides. There is research suggesting that the heart sends more neurological information to the brain through the vagus nerve than the brain sends to the heart.[1] So, the key insight here is that more sensations travel from the heart and body to the brain than the other way around. Through these exercises, you aren't using logic to create a purpose statement. You are allowing your heart to reveal it to your mind.

After completing each exercise, you'll jot down three words that resonate most deeply with you based on your reflections. These words may represent feelings, values, passions, or key insights that emerged during the exercise. By the end of all three exercises, you'll have a collection of nine words or ideas that reflect your inner core. These words serve as tools for crafting your Higher Purpose statement. Essentially, you will be distilling what you gained from each exercise down to three words, allowing you to align feeling with language.

You may notice patterns emerge. For example, if when you reflect on joy or your ideal day you find yourself feeling *creativity*, *freedom*, or *leadership*, it means these things are deeply important to you. They aren't just random thoughts. They are what truly lights you up inside.

It's also just as fine if, during each exercise, you write down completely different words. These words name different parts of your vibration. When you choose a word for a feeling or sensation that emerges from the exercises, your heart and brain are in sync. Remember, your purpose is already present within you. It is not something you invent. It is something you uncover. The words you gather simply help you name it.

From the nine words you gather after completing all three steps, you will choose three final words. With these three words in hand, you'll draft your Higher Purpose statement.

If in the end you want to assess your Higher Purpose statement through a helpful framework, you can always refer to the previous chapter to revisit the stages of Dharma to see what stages are present in your statement. But as mentioned earlier, although the tools and philosophy discussed in the previous chapter are there to inspire and guide you, your final statement should come from you, not from a mold. Approach these steps with curiosity, patience, and openness. Allow yourself to dive deep, explore freely, and uncover what makes you feel most alive.

Visionary Practice: Remembering Your Story of Joy

This exercise helps you reflect on a moment of pure joy from your past, such as a time when you felt ecstatic, delighted, or completely present. You will gain insight into the experiences that bring you deep fulfillment.

Take a Moment to Ground Yourself

If this feels right to you, pause before beginning and ask a Higher Power, Source, or any aspect of Spirit that resonates with you to assist you in this exercise. Ask for this Visionary Practice to be a successful undertaking that will lead you to uncover your Higher Purpose.

Guidelines

Recall a peak moment of joy from your past. Think of a time when you felt the greatest excitement or fulfillment, one that stands out above all others. It might be a fun childhood memory, a celebration of a professional achievement, a time in nature, a creative breakthrough, or a moment of deep connection with someone you love.

Write a story about what happened. Describe this moment in as much detail as possible, bringing it to life on the page. As you write, consider:

- the what, where, when, why, who, and how of the experience
- emotions that rose within you

- Why does this moment stand out?
- What did this experience teach you about yourself, about life, or about what truly matters?

If one story doesn't feel like enough, you can write about multiple moments that brought you similar joy. Sometimes, the pattern between them is just as revealing as the experiences themselves.

After, pause for a moment. Connect with your inner experience. Step back and read your story again. Reflect on the following questions:

- Beyond what happened, what was the deeper feeling underneath this joy?
- What made this moment so meaningful?
- What does this memory tell you about the kind of joy that feels most natural and fulfilling to you?

Identify Three Defining Words

What three words capture the essence of your story of joy? Delve into the feeling and sensations that you felt while writing or reading your narrative. Try to name those feelings in three words. As you choose your words, notice how each one feels. In finding the right words, you are aligning a high vibration with language.

Visionary Practice: Imagining Your Ideal Day

This exercise invites you to envision a typical day in a future where everything in your life is perfect. Envision yourself fully realized, meaning you have already fulfilled all of your life's biggest ambitions. This will allow you to gain information from the Witnessing State rather than the Ego State because in this imagined future, you will not be pursuing anything, rather you will be in a high state of fulfillment.

Take a Moment to Ground Yourself

If this feels right to you, pause before beginning and ask a Higher Power, Source, or any aspect of Spirit that resonates with you to assist you in this exercise. Ask for this Visionary Practice to be a successful undertaking that will lead you to uncover your Higher Purpose.

Guidelines

Visualize a typical day in a perfect future, where you are fully accomplished and have made all of your dreams come true. You have unlimited financial resources, perfect health, and abundant time. All obstacles that might otherwise limit you have been eliminated.

This is not about imagining an unattainable fantasy but about identifying the deeper themes that bring you fulfillment. What truly matters to you when nothing is holding you back? Describe your day in detail, covering what happens hour by hour, from the moment you wake up to when you go to sleep. As you write, consider:

- the what, where, when, why, and who, of the experience
- What is the first thing that you do?
- What activities fill your morning, afternoon, and evening?
- How do you feel throughout each phase of your day?

Use rich details to bring your vision to life.

After, pause for a moment. Connect with your inner experience. As you read over your ideal day, look beyond external accomplishments or material success. Reflect on the following questions:

- What thoughts or feelings define this day?
- What aspects of this day feel most alive in your body?

Identify Three Defining Words

What three words capture the essence of your story of joy? Delve into the feeling and sensations that you felt while writing or reading your narrative. Try to name those feelings in three words. As you choose your words, notice how each one feels. In finding the right words, you are aligning a high vibration with language.

Visionary Practice: Who Am I? Meditation

This meditation is designed to help you clear your thoughts as much as possible so you can arrive at a deeper layer within your mind where you can focus on your own consciousness. This practice will use breathing techniques to guide you inward, clearing out mental chatter and helping you focus your mind on inner connection. The idea is to quiet your mind, so you can hear information that comes directly from pure consciousness. Be patient with yourself if you are not perfect at this. Experienced meditators practice meditation over lifetimes to arrive at a pure state of settled consciousness. Trust in the outcome of your effort.

Take a Moment to Ground Yourself

If this feels right to you, pause before beginning and ask a Higher Power, Source, or any aspect of Spirit that resonates with you to assist you in this exercise. Ask for this Visionary Practice to be a successful undertaking that will lead you to uncover your Higher Purpose.

Step One: Grounding and Calling in Support. Take a moment to find a comfortable position, whether seated or lying down, and close your eyes. Begin by noticing the natural rhythm of your breath. Feel the rise and fall of your chest. Take a deep breath in through your nose, allowing your chest and belly to expand, and exhale gently through your mouth. Repeat this three times, letting each exhalation melt away tension and distractions.

Step Two: Intentional Breathing. Bring your attention fully to your breath. Begin a steady rhythm: inhale deeply for three seconds through your nose and exhale slowly for four seconds through your mouth.

Inhale for one... two... three... and exhale for one... two... three... four...

As you continue this rhythm, imagine each inhalation filling you with clarity and light, and each exhalation releasing what no longer serves you. Let your breath anchor you in the present moment, drawing you inward with each cycle.

If your mind wanders, gently bring your focus back to the steady rhythm of your breath. Don't rush through this moment. Feel your mind settle with each breath. As described in a previous chapter, witness yourself move from the Survival or Ego State to the Witnessing State or the Infinite Soul State. Remain in a silent state, observing your breath or consciousness for a while longer.

Step Three: Holding the Question and Feeling the Answer. Now, bring the question "Who am I?" into your awareness. As you continue your breathing, let the question settle deeply within you, without rushing to answer it.

With each inhalation, invite clarity to arise. With each exhalation, let go of expectations or the need to force an answer.

Bring your awareness to your body. Notice any sensations, emotions, or shifts as you hold the question. The answer may come as a word, an image, a memory, or simply a feeling that arises from your body. Allow yourself to sense it fully, trusting whatever emerges.

Repeat the question silently: "Who am I?" and listen. Feel the answer come not just from your mind but also from your heart, your body, and your soul.

Step Four: Closing. When you are ready, slowly bring your awareness back to the room. Notice the ground beneath you. Begin to wiggle your fingers and toes. Take one final deep breath. Thank Source, or the Higher Power you called upon, for the connection and self-discovery you gained. Then, gently open your eyes.

After, pause for a moment. Write down what came to you during the meditation.

Identify Three Defining Words

Now, step back and reflect on your writing. What words, sensations, or feelings arose? Review your notes and distill the essence of your insights into three words that resonate most deeply with you.

Visionary Practice: Revealing Who You Really Are

You are now ready to draft a Higher Purpose statement that serves as a foundation for growth and intentional living. More than just a sentence or phrase, it is a source of inspiration, guiding you toward a cohesive ideology for your highest good. This will also be the first code you inscribe in your Higher Purpose Codex.

As I mentioned earlier, your Higher Purpose is not something you create from nothing; it is something already within you, waiting to be uncovered. Think of a sculptor working with a block of stone. The image they seek is already inside. The sculptor's job is simply to remove what is unnecessary to reveal it. In the same way, your purpose has always been within you. The process of discovering it is not about building something new but about clearing away distractions, doubts, and external expectations, so you can see what has been there all along.

Take a Moment to Ground Yourself

If this feels right to you, pause before beginning and ask a Higher Power, Source, or any aspect of Spirit that resonates with you to assist you in this exercise. Ask for this Visionary Practice to be a successful undertaking that will lead you to uncover your Higher Purpose.

Step One: Grounding. Drafting your Higher Purpose statement will be enhanced if you are operating from your highest level of awareness. So, as you approach this exercise, I encourage you to evaluate what level of awareness you are currently at as you begin drafting your statement.

Do you feel agitated or calm? If you're unsure which state you're operating from, reread the earlier sections that explain them in more detail. Refer to the meditation guide in the Who am I? Meditation practice to center yourself, if necessary, and bring your mind into either the Witnessing state or Infinite Soul state. This will help you connect deeply with your intuition as you move forward. Your Higher Purpose statement will resonate more deeply if it comes from a calm, centered mind rather than a place of anxiety or external pressure.

Step Two: Choosing Your Language. Have the sets of three words you identified in the previous exercises in hand. You should now have a total of nine words you gathered from these exercises. Arrange these words in front of you, either physically or digitally, so you can observe all of them. These words represent key feelings, themes, or values that emerged through your reflections. Select the final three that resonate most deeply with you.

Choose the words that evoke a strong emotional or physical responses inside you. Pay attention to the goosebumps you might feel with each word or other sensations in your body. Choose the ones that are the most meaningful to you.

Step Three: Writing the First Code. Using the final three words, start building your Higher Purpose Codex and draft the first code. Begin with:

Code One
My Higher Purpose is...

Sample
using the words *humility*, *compassion*, and *integrity*:

My Higher Purpose is to be of service to others with humility, compassion, and integrity to the best of my capacity. Through presence, listening, and action, I strive to be of service, especially to those who are disempowered, so I can help to build a better world.

Your purpose statement should reflect your unique nature. There is no right or wrong way to do this. Your statement can be as long or as short as you like. What matters is that it feels right to you. You should feel a sense of energy, clarity, or enthusiasm when you read it. The word enthusiasm comes from the Greek *Entheos*, meaning inspired or possessed by God. Your Higher Purpose statement should spark something within you. It should feel alive. If your statement makes you feel uncertain or uninspired, you may need to refine it further.

Step Four: Reflecting. You now have a draft of a Higher Purpose statement. Reflect on its significance and practical application in your life. Consider the following points, and write your reflections in your journal:

- On a scale of 1 to 10, how happy are you with the statement you created? Why did you rate it this way?
- How can you use this statement in your daily life right now?
- How accurately does this statement capture your unique essence today?
- How might this statement help you when facing challenges?

- How can this statement serve as a compass
  to help you make better decisions?

Throughout the next two weeks, revisit these questions to see if your Higher Purpose statement needs to be adjusted. Feel free to make as many changes as you like.

Step Five: Turning Your Higher Purpose Into Inquiry. Rather than seeing your Higher Purpose as a fixed answer, consider turning it into an ongoing question. This can help you remain engaged with your purpose and help you brainstorm ways to carry it forward. For example, if your statement is—*My Higher Purpose is to nurture heartfelt leadership that fosters a culture of sustainability and collective inspiration*— this can lead to deep questions like:

- What does it mean to be a leader from the heart?
- What does a sustainable culture truly look like?
- How can I work more collaboratively
  to inspire the collective?

Answering these questions will inspire you to action and keep you engaged in fulfilling your purpose.

Step Six: Dharma and Your Higher Purpose (Optional). Reflect on Vistara, Rasa, and Seva. How does your purpose statement align with each one?

Vistara (Expansion). How does your Higher Purpose reflect growth and learning?

Rasa (Adaptability and Flow). Does the scope of your purpose help you embrace life's challenges with grace, resilience, and adaptability?

Seva (Selfless Service). How does your Higher Purpose uplift others, foster connection, or contribute to the greater good?

Your statement doesn't need to necessarily refer to each of these principles. These stages are referenced to help you create a purpose that is expansive, balanced, and compassionate.

By completing these steps, you will gain a clear and empowering statement. Don't be surprised if your Higher Purpose feels a little mysterious at first. In time, greater clarity will emerge. Trust that you received true knowledge if you worked from your highest level of awareness.

MILESTONE MARKER. Congratulations! If you have successfully written your Higher Purpose statement, then you have accomplished the first milestone in our book, which is to write your first code in your Higher Purpose Codex. Fantastic job! Cue the band to celebrate your accomplishment.

Part Two

Your Core Values

Invitation

"Don't Be Evil"

IN THE EARLY DAYS OF GOOGLE, its code of conduct began with three unforgettable words: "Don't be evil." It was a phrase that made people believe Google was more than just another profit-seeking corporation. It painted the picture of a modern, innovative company committed to doing good in the world, setting itself apart from competitors who seemed driven only by money. But when the motto was quietly retired in 2015, it raised a harder question: if even the world's most admired innovators cannot hold on to their own values, what does that mean for the rest of us?[1]

Walk into almost any organization, whether it's a global corporation, a small nonprofit, or a local yoga studio, and you'll likely find a list of "Core Values" posted on the wall. These are often guiding principles like integrity, innovation, inclusion, or service. At their best, these values aren't just words. They can shape culture, influence decisions, and remind the organization of what it stands for. At their worst, they risk becoming empty slogans that sound good but fail to translate into action.

What about you as an individual? What would it look like for you to live by a set of Core Values? The values I am referring to here are moral values—the kind that shape your character. They are not about winning approval or optimizing efficiency. Instead, they are about becoming the purest, grounded, and most benevolent version of yourself, such as:

- offering kindness when it's easier to withdraw
- setting boundaries and respect the boundaries of others
- speaking with compassion
- choosing humility over arrogance, love over fear, and service over self-interest

Core Values are ultimately practical commitments. They enable you to walk through the world causing less pain and spreading the most joy.

Many single people have a list of external tactics they use to attract an ideal partner: a good credit score or a fancy car. They do not, however, have a list of qualities they endeavor to possess within themselves to help them nurture a relationship. Part two of this book invites you to make that list.

What Does It Mean to Do "Good"?

Let's be honest. In today's world, talking about becoming your *purest self* might sound a little corny. We live in a culture that often rewards cleverness over kindness, success over sincerity, and image over integrity. In some circles, trying to be "good" is even dismissed as naive—something for Buddhist monks, or people who haven't faced the "real world." But for many of us, it is important to discard this kind of cynicism for the sake of feeling at peace with ourselves. We understand that how we do things matters. I want to show you that this ideal doesn't come from weakness; it comes from wisdom.

So, what does it really mean to be good, and why should we even try? Being good isn't about being perfect. It's not about always saying the right thing or never making mistakes. Goodness is not a performance. It's who we are at our best, and it carries a commitment to live with conscience, courage, and care—even when it's inconvenient.

To be good is to ask:

- Am I living in alignment with what I know to be right?
- Am I treating others the way I hope to be treated?
- Am I becoming someone whom people can depend on?

These questions don't require grand gestures. They invite small acts of integrity: a kind word instead of a harsh truth, a thought of goodwill toward competitors, or a commitment to personal growth, even when you fail.

Doing good heals. It builds inner strength and draws people to you because they feel safe in your presence. More importantly, doing good leads to real inner peace.

Cultivating a Moral Base

To live a moral life, not in a religious, dogmatic sense, but in the spirit of being good, can be your strongest foundation. What good would it do to own a profitable business if unethical actions will bring about your downfall in lawsuits or debt? All of your best achievements can crumble beneath you if you are not standing on a solid, principled base, where you know good from bad. In fact, you need a solid moral base for some of the most important areas of life.

To raise a healthy family, you need more than money. You need patience, loyalty, and humility. Children learn how to live in society through the values they learn in the home. Similarly, to build a meaningful career, you need values that keep you honest when money, power, or competition try to pull you off course. To carry out your Higher Purpose, morality is essential. A strong mission without morals can become ego-driven, manipulative, and even destructive.

On the spiritual path, morality is not the décor for the house. It is the foundation. Baba wrote in the opening line of his 1957 book, *Guide to Human Conduct*, "Morality is the foundation of *sadhana*, (spiritual practice)." As your inner life deepens, so does your capacity to affect the world around you. Spiritual growth brings spiritual power, and sometimes other benefits such as a sharpened intuition, a charismatic presence, and authority over others. Yet, without a moral compass, that power can turn toxic and can lead to abuse and violence.

History and news headlines are filled with examples of charismatic spiritual teachers who gained power but lost their way, allegedly using their gifts to exploit, deceive, or manipulate others. Their downfall wasn't caused by a lack of vision. It was caused by a lack of a morals guiding their actions. Morality is what keeps your spiritual power rooted in humility, your leadership aligned with service, and your relationships grounded in trust.

The Ethical Values of Yoga: *Yama* and *Niyama*

One of the most beautiful frameworks for cultivating moral clarity comes from the yogic tradition: the ten principles of Yama and Niyama. These foundational principles, passed down through thousands of years, offer a powerful ethical structure for anyone walking a path of growth and self-discovery. The Yamas are ethical restraints—five principles that guide how you relate to others. The Niyamas are personal observances—five practices that help you develop discipline, clarity, and alignment with your higher self. Collectively, they offer universal wisdom.

But how you live them is entirely personal. Your values, like your purpose, are not fixed in stone. You are not expected to live them perfectly, only to live them consciously—to revisit them, question them, and recommit to them as life throws its challenges at you. Before we explore each of the principles of Yama and Niyama, take a moment to reflect on the values have guided you in the past. Are they still relevant today? Where did they come from, and how do they make you feel when you are true to them?

Moral values emerge from many sources: sacred texts, lived experiences, and cultural roots. Some of your values may have been shaped by the Ten Commandments or the teachings of the Qur'an. Others may have arisen through personal experience from childhood, moments of grief, or from moments of redemption, such as serving time behind bars.

In the next ten chapters, we will explore each of the Yamas and Niyamas as invitations for you to reflect, refine, and redefine your personal values. Sharing these principles is not about fitting you into a mold or forcing you to adopt someone else's moral code. They are opportunities to notice what resonates, what is good, and what feels true.

The Yamas guide how you can live in harmony with the world around you:

- non-harming in words, thoughts, or actions (*Ahimsa*)
- speaking with compassion (*Satya*)
- non-stealing (*Asteya*)
- seeing everything as an expression of the Divine (*Brahmacharya*).
- living simply and non-hoarding (*Aparigraha*)

The Niyamas, on the other hand, guide how you can create harmony within yourself:

- mental and physical cleanliness (*Shaocha*)
- contentment (*Santosha*)
- selfless service (*Tapah*)
- spiritual study (*Svadhyaya*)
- accelerated spiritual growth (*Iishvara Pranidhana*)

As you move through each one, I encourage you to record the words, phrases, or insights that stand out to you. You may want to start creating a Core Values list, tracking the themes that feel most aligned with who you want to become. Strive for alignment between your Core Values and your Higher Purpose.

In my own life, the Yamas and Niyamas have been particularly transformational, especially the way Baba interprets them in his book *Guide to Human Conduct* (1957). Some of the stories and the way the principles are taught in the next ten chapters mirrors his book. I invite you to read *Guide to Human Conduct* for deeper exploration.

There's one last point I would like to share with you before diving into the ten principles. During my life coaching training, Gustavo Prudente shared that Core Values are like the protective membrane of a cell that surrounds its nucleus. Just as the membrane shields the nucleus preventing unwanted elements to enter, your Core Values shield you from actions or influences that go against your truth.

Visionary Practice: Holding Space for Your Core Values

This week, set the intention for building the next phase of your Higher Purpose Codex. Ask the Universe to make clear in your mind your Core Values. Ask for the wisdom to know what is good and what you can practice for more harmony with yourself and others.

Perhaps you can take five - ten flowers to a nearby mountain or lake and offer each one from your heart in exchange for the awareness of a moral principle. As another act of reciprocity, consider giving something back to the Earth, such as planting seeds in the soil or removing trash from the ground. You can also make a promise—the promise to make the world a better place through your values. Make an offering and invite something beautiful into your life.

Living Without Harm:
The Heart of *Ahimsa*

"If you can, help others. If you cannot, at least do not harm them."
— *Dalai Lama XIV, Ethics for the New Millennium*

THE TIMELESS CORE VALUE OF NON-HARMING is called Ahimsa (uh-HIM-sah) in Sanskrit. It reminds us to live with compassion and integrity. At its core, Ahimsa means avoiding harm, not just in actions but also in words and thoughts. It's about seeking to minimize pain and promote the well-being of all life forms, whether human or more-than-human.

Non-harming is often misunderstood. Many equate it with nonviolence, believing it forbids any force. But what about in cases of self-defense? Protecting oneself or the vulnerable from abuse or aggression isn't a violation of Ahimsa. Rather, I believe it is an application of it.

Imagine a mother bird defending her chicks from a predator. This can hardly be called acting violently. Similarly, even anger when resisting oppression aligns with non-harming when it arises from a place of justice. The principle doesn't ask us to remain passive in the face of harm. Instead, Ahimsa calls us to act in ways that reduce suffering and protect the vulnerable.

Living With Compassion

Throughout history, people have twisted the concept of non-harming to serve their own ends. For instance, in ancient India some religious individuals attempted to practice non-harming by avoiding plowing fields to prevent killing insects in the soil. Yet, they delegated this task to servants of lower castes. While they may have kept their hands clean, they pushed the dirty work onto others.

While the actions of these individuals can easily be dismissed as motivated by selfishness, they do reveal an apparent contradiction in the concept of Ahimsa: perfect non-harming is impossible. Even the simple act of breathing has the potential to kill microscopic life forms in our respiratory system. But this is not a real contradiction, because non-harming doesn't demand perfection. It asks us to be conscious and compassionate with our actions to the best of our ability. The central question for those who wish to practice non-harming is: How can I live in a way that causes the least amount of pain?

Take food choices, for example. A tomato, lacking a nervous system, seemingly feels less pain, while animals like cows and chickens experience visible suffering when killed for food. For some, choosing plant-based options can align more closely with non-harming. Even those who eat meat can strive toward greater compassion by choosing sources that prioritize animal welfare, such as grass-fed livestock raised in more humane conditions.

But the consumption of meat, and even abstaining from eating meat, is not always so straightforward. In many parts of the world, vegetarian diets are becoming more accessible. Still, for some Indigenous communities, hunting remains a vital tradition. For some Native peoples in the United States, carrying on traditional hunting practices symbolizes resilience and autonomy after centuries of cultural erasure and forced assimilation. In these contexts, such practices embody survival and justice, not indulgence. While harm cannot always be eliminated, traditional Indigenous harvesting and hunting practices can reduce suffering, often reflecting a deeper respect for all living beings.

Non-harming extends far beyond diet. Consider fashion choices. Buying clothing made through exploitative labor harms workers and communities. Supporting union labor and sustainable, ethical brands reduces harm and helps to preserve resources on Earth. Every choice we make—how we travel, what we consume, and how we interact with others—is an opportunity to practice non-harming and ethical living.

Perhaps the most overlooked aspect of Ahimsa lies in our thoughts. Every action begins with a thought. For example, harboring resentment or ill-will can snowball into harmful actions. Conversely, replacing negative thoughts toward others with compassionate thoughts can change how we approach conflict and breed positive actions.

To practice non-harming is to embrace the interconnectedness of all life. It means wishing for the happiness and protection of human beings and more-than-human beings. Whether it's choosing to walk instead of drive to reduce pollution, rescuing an injured bird, or speaking up for someone being mistreated, every small act of non-harming contributes to a larger web of kindness. As mentioned above, Ahimsa doesn't ask us to be perfect. It asks us to behave as kindly as possible. It challenges us to think, to feel, and to act with care, ensuring that the impact we leave behind causes the least amount of pain wherever we go.

Truth with Kindness:
The Practice of *Satya*

COMPASSIONATE SPEAKING, OR SATYA (SUT-yah), refers to the benevolent and intentional use of words with the aim of creating the highest good. Practicing this principle means speaking in a way that uplifts, protects, and serves the well-being of others. It also means engaging with an essential part of our humanity. In *Guide to Human Conduct* (1957), Baba explains, "Humans are rational beings. They possess, in varying degrees, the capability to do what is necessary or good for humanity."[1] One dimension within our control is how we choose our words.

Imagine living during the era of slavery in the United States. An enslaved woman, who has escaped her captors, arrives at your door in desperate need for shelter. You agree to take her in and offer her comfort. Shortly after, the slave master appears, demanding to know her whereabouts. What would compassionate speaking entail in this situation?

While the Biblical commandment, "Thou shalt not lie," might suggest divulging the slave's whereabouts, this would effectively betray the runaway and subject her to torture and punishment. Instead, the compassionate response would be to lie. You might claim to have never seen the enslaved woman and even provide misleading information to divert the slave master's search to protect the runaway. In this case, your intentional misdirection is an example of Satya.

The example above illustrates how compassionate speaking sometimes requires bending conventional rules of truth-telling to uphold a higher moral standard. This is not to say that one should favor lying over speaking truth. In many interpersonal relationships, lying and deceit often cause deep pain, damaging trust. Satya emphasizes benevolent truthfulness—a balance between honesty and kindness.

Consider another example of compassionate speaking. Esperanza and Miguel are an immigrant couple living in the United States. One evening, Miguel receives a call from Esperanza's father, still living in her home country. He has devastating news for the couple—Esperanza's mother passed away unexpectedly. Her father, deeply saddened but wanting to ensure his daughter receives the news with support, asks Miguel to tell Esperanza in person rather than over the phone. Miguel is now faced with how to tell Esperanza the difficult news. Should he immediately share the news as soon as Esperanza walks in? If Miguel were to deliver such shocking information abruptly, Esperanza might be too overwhelmed. She may not eat out of sadness.

Instead, Miguel creates a calm and supportive environment, while waiting for Esperanza to come home. He prepares dinner and hides his own grief to make sure she is well fed and stable. He prepares her favorite tea and invites her to sit in a quiet, comfortable space where she feels safe. Miguel starts by holding Esperanza's hands and gently saying, "I need to talk to you about something important. Your father called me earlier." He pauses, giving Esperanza a moment to prepare herself emotionally. Then, with a steady and comforting tone, he gradually shares the circumstances that led to her mother's death, giving Esperanza time to process the information little by little. As Esperanza takes in the difficult news, Miguel stays by her side, holding her and offering support.

By delivering the news in this thoughtful and loving manner, both Miguel and Esperanza's father demonstrate the essence of compassionate speaking. Their approach not only softens the blow but also reassures Esperanza that she is not alone, deepening their bond as they face the loss together.

In daily interactions, too, words can heal or harm, build bridges or walls. For example, gently explaining a difficult truth to a friend, rather than coldly pointing out their flaws, fosters care and respect. Similarly, when it comes to parenting, lovingly explaining a child's mistake while emphasizing their potential for growth teaches accountability without damaging self-esteem. In the workplace, a manager offering constructive criticism in a respectful and encouraging tone can inspire improvement rather than resentment among employees.

Satya's Effect on the Collective

On a societal level, the principles of honesty related to Satya are just as critical. When politicians or leaders lie out of convenience, public trust is eroded, leading to disillusionment with democratic institutions and political apathy. Conversely, when governments and public figures practice honesty and transparency, citizens are empowered to make informed decisions. Imagine the harm politicians would be responsible for had they chosen to deprive people of understanding the gravity of the COVID-19 pandemic in the name of avoiding shutdowns. People would not have been able to adequately protect themselves and their loved ones during the early spread of the virus.

As we have seen, the practice of compassionate speaking is crucial both in large situations and in the home. Compassionate speaking is about using language to serve the greater good. It requires empathy and a commitment to the welfare of others, making it a cornerstone for meaningful relationships.

Building a World Without Theft: The Wisdom of *Asteya*

WHEN I WAS A YOUNG BOY, I lived in a house with bars across every window in a neighborhood in Bolivia. The bars weren't decorations. They were for protection. In fact, every house on our street had them because theft was so common. No one felt safe leaving a window uncovered. I remember my grandmother grieving after someone broke into her home one morning when she was out getting food from the market. I also remember neighbors complaining about someone's bicycle being gone, someone's stereo taken. It was common for wallets to be pulled while walking around crowded places.

Even as a child, I could feel the tension. You learned to clutch your belongings tightly, to mistrust strangers, and even to look suspiciously at your friends. Looking back, I have realized that theft didn't just take objects. It took away something far more valuable: trust.

Imagine just for a moment the world turned upside down—life without theft. We could lend a tool to a neighbor and know it would return. In yoga, the principle of non-stealing is known as Asteya (uh-STAY-yah). It's rooted in a universal truth: no one likes their belongings taken from them. Although theft can be attributed to complex factors, including societal inequalities, we each play a role in controlling our behavior to not take what does not belong to us.

Different Kinds of Theft

Though this principle may seem straightforward at first glance, my guru identified four distinct kinds of theft in his book *Guide to Human Conduct* (1957), each worth understanding and reflecting upon.

Physical Theft

This is the most obvious form of stealing. It is taking someone else's property without their consent. For example, walking into a convenience store and pocketing an item without paying for it.

Mental Theft

This occurs when we imagine taking something without permission, even if we do not act on the thought. For instance, in a crowded marketplace, a person might see a distracted vendor and think, "I could easily take this shirt right now, and no one would notice." Though no action is taken, the thought itself reflects a tendency toward dishonesty. Such mental tendencies, if unchecked, can weaken one's ethical foundation.

Depriving Others of Their Due

According to Baba, "Even if you do not take possession of what belongs to others, but you deprive others of what is their due, you become responsible for their loss." Examples include delaying repayment of a loan or withholding fair wages from workers. Employers who exploit their employees through unfair compensation are as guilty of theft as someone who steals physical goods.

Mentally Depriving Others of Their Due

This form of theft involves plotting to cheat someone out of what is rightfully theirs. Consider a home-buyer who, at the last minute, points out minor flaws in a house to justify offering ten percent less than the agreed-upon price. While this action may seem shrewd, it is rooted in dishonesty and contributes to harmful business practices. Such thinking fosters greed and selfishness, which erodes trust in society.

Theft of All Sizes and Types

Acts of theft can be found in both minor and major forms. A mother might lie about her child's age to get a cheaper ticket or concertgoers might pay for inexpensive seats but sneak into premium sections. These seemingly harmless actions are still forms of cheating that instill dishonesty in the person committing the acts.

On a larger scale, individuals or groups use advanced methods of stealing that involve modern technology. For instance, the CNN-reported case of a finance worker being duped into transferring $25.6 million to fraudsters using deepfake technology highlights the increasing sophistication of theft.[1] The story showed that scammers simulated a realistic video conference to impersonate a multinational firm's CFO to execute their scheme. Financial scams like this reveal how vulnerable individuals are to digital deception, and the increasing sophistication of technology means its misuse has graver consequences. At worst, modern technology could be used as a weapon of infiltration and even surveillance.

On a governmental scale, theft is used as a tool for power and control. As journalist Ronan Farrow reported in *The New Yorker*, governments, with the help of companies like Pegasus, use spyware to gain access to people's devices and data without their consent.[2] This allows them to steal private information, monitor conversations, and track locations, often targeting journalists, activists, and political opponents. These actions are large-scale acts of digital theft and manipulation, which violate privacy and basic human rights.

From the interpersonal to intergovernmental level, practicing non-stealing requires a commitment to self-restraint and integrity. Ultimately, Asteya challenges us to go beyond mere avoidance of theft. It asks us to cultivate a sense of mental purity in which we act with fairness and generosity in all our dealings. In doing so, we contribute to a world where trust and mutual respect can thrive.

The True Meaning of *Brahmacharya*

ONE DAY, A YOUNG MAN NAMED RAMESH was walking through the marketplace in a small town in India, when he saw an old beggar sitting on the roadside. The beggar was dirty, frail, and muttered to himself. Disgusted, Ramesh tried to ignore him and quickened his pace, thinking, *What use could that beggar possibly have in this world?*

Years passed, and Ramesh encountered a natural disaster. A devastating flood swept through his village, leaving him houseless and desperate. Struggling to find shelter, he wandered until he reached the same marketplace he had once walked through so proudly. To his surprise, he found refuge in a small tent set up by a group offering food and care to those in need. Among the helpers was the very beggar he had dismissed years earlier. Recognizing the man, Ramesh hung his head in shame. The old beggar, now with a spark of vitality in his eyes, smiled and said, "You see, life has a way of teaching us that no one is useless. Just as you needed me today, someone will need you tomorrow. We are all threads in the divine tapestry of life."

Many times, we make the mistake of writing people off, forgetting that every person carries within them the potential to touch our life in a positive way. Taking this a step further, we can learn not only to see the good in all, but to see the Divine in all, which is the true meaning of the principle of Brahmacharya (BRAH-mah-CHAR-yah).

People often misunderstand the practice of Brahmacharya in the world of yoga. While some associate it with sexual abstinence, its true meaning is far more profound and expansive. Where does the misconception stem from? According to Baba, historically, certain groups, particularly priests, emphasized sexual abstinence as a marker of spiritual superiority.[1] This led to the misconception that Brahmacharya is solely about restraint in this area. While discipline, including in matters of sexuality, has its place, Brahmacharya is about perceiving and honoring the Divine in all aspects of existence.

From the point of view of the average person, everything outside of them seems external, separate, and finite. Yet yoga philosophy teaches us that from the point of view of Brahma or God, all things are internal thought-waves, even what humans perceive to be physical and solid. This realization transforms our understanding of everything in the Universe. When we recognize that all beings, objects, and phenomena are manifestations or thought waves in this cosmic mind, we see that everything is interconnected and divine.

As Baba explains in *Guide to Human Conduct* (1957), "The meaning of practicing Brahmacharya is to treat the objects with which one comes into contact as different expressions of Brahma, not as crude forms." In other words, Brahmacharya is the practice of seeing through the apparent physicality of things and recognizing their deeper, divine essence. This perspective fosters a sense of unity with the Divine and a profound respect for all of creation.

Consider this analogy: imagine being invited to stay at a grand royal palace. The beauty and elegance of the furnishings, the fine linens, polished silverware, and exquisite decor reflect the grandeur and magnitude of the host. As a guest, you naturally feel a sense of reverence and gratitude, taking great care not to damage anything out of respect. In the same way, the world is Brahma or God's palace. Every person, animal, plant, and even mineral is part of His divine household.

When we see all things as belonging to the Divine, we approach life with humility and reverence, treating every interaction as sacred. This awareness allows us to flow through life as caretakers, honoring and preserving the interconnected web of existence. Living in this way not only deepens our connection to the spiritual world but also transforms our relationships and interactions, allowing us to move through life with reverence.

Seeing the Divine in all calls us to honor the sacredness in others, even when it is not immediately apparent. Like Ramesh, we are often quick to judge or dismiss those we encounter, forgetting that everyone has a role to play in the unfolding of life. The beggar who seems irrelevant today may be the person who saves us tomorrow. With this is mind, we can see that every person we meet has something to teach us.

The End of Excess: Practicing *Aparigraha*

SHOULD BILLIONAIRES EXIST? This is a question that sparks heated debates around the world. After all, no single person could ever need a yacht, a private jet, or dozens of houses. Further, when a small, exalted number of people control vast amounts of the world's resources, it perpetuates inequality. Yet, billionaires are the result of an economic system and culture that celebrates, accumulation. Though on a smaller scale, many of us, not just billionaires, fall into the same trap of chasing more than we truly need.

Living simply and letting go of excess, known as Aparigraha (ah-PAH-ree-GRAH-hah) in Sanskrit, means avoiding unnecessary accumulation. It encourages us to focus on what we truly need instead of seeking extra comforts or possessions that aren't essential for daily life. Human desire is limitless, meaning no material object can fulfill our inner needs indefinitely. A new fancy object is lots of fun on the first day you get it, but its excitement soon dies down in just a matter of days, reducing itself to just another mundane object in your home. Aparigraha reminds us that lasting fulfillment does not come from consumption, but from learning to be content with what truly sustains us.

Indigenous peoples around the world have long embodied the principle of contentment through living simply, often inhabiting simple dwellings and being guided by a deep respect for nature. Their way of life shows that true fulfillment does not come from material accumulation but from harmony with the land, community, and Spirit. For many Indigenous cultures, the idea of "ownership" differs vastly from the materialistic perspective prevalent in modern Western societies. Rather than hoarding resources or accumulating wealth, they view land, water, and natural resources as sacred gifts to be shared and stewarded, not exploited or possessed. An Indigenous worldview encourages sufficiency, where people take only what they need and ensure resources remain available for future generations.

Individual and Collective Approaches to Simplicity

On an individual level, practicing simplicity begins with tempered consumption. This involves evaluating whether possessions or purchases serve a genuine need or merely satisfy fleeting desires. For example, instead of spending money on the latest smartphone every year, one might choose to use devices until they are no longer functional. By embracing simplicity, you may shift your values from external markers of success, such as wealth or luxury items, to internal growth, such as learning new skills, pursuing creative hobbies, or deepening spiritual practice. When you consume only what you need, you free up resources for others, contribute to a more equitable world, and lower the demand for unnecessary production.

On a societal level, Aparigraha challenges us to question systems that allow the extreme accumulation of wealth while others suffer from scarcity. The existence of billionaires, individuals whose wealth surpasses what they could possibly spend in multiple lifetimes, stands in stark contrast to the principle of living simply and letting go of excess.

Billionaire wealth often comes at a collective cost. Companies that generate such immense fortunes frequently do so by exploiting labor, evading taxes, and depleting natural resources. These practices undermine the stability of communities and ecosystems. The hoarding of wealth by billionaires not only merges economic and political power in the hands of a few but also may deprive others of the resources needed to make food, housing, education, and healthcare accessible to all. The case for abolishing billionaires actually speaks to the importance of living simply and letting go of excess, pointing to the collective crisis created when wealth is concentrated in the hands of the few.

Adjusting to Your Own Needs

Living simply and letting go of excess is not a one-size-fits-all principle. People's needs vary based on their circumstances, cultural context, and the era in which they live. What was considered a luxury a century ago, such as owning a telephone, is now a basic utility. In modern households, it is reasonable for each family member to have their own phone. This was not the case just 30 years ago. As technology advances, new "necessities" may emerge, making it essential not to be dogmatic about the practice of Aparigraha.

Living simply does not mean rejecting comfort or progress; rather, it means practicing moderation and rational use of resources. The key is balance—consuming only what is necessary while ensuring the needs of others are met. It's also important to acknowledge that individuals should get to moderate their personal needs, consumption, and habits, without being imposed on heavily.

However, decisions that affect the entire society, such as immense accumulation at the expense of the collective, should be made democratically. In this sense, Aparigraha encourages us to think about what interventions can be organized through a system of economic democracy, where people can vote on economic issues. For example, imagine if you could vote on what the minimum wage should be or what the cap on wealth should be. You would have a lot more power to balance wealth inequality in your society. By adopting an ethic of simplicity, individuals and societies alike can address harmful disparities.

As Mahatma Gandhi famously said, "The world has enough for everyone's needs, but not for everyone's greed."[1] Aparigraha calls on us to reflect deeply on what we truly require, both as individuals and as a collective. By practicing simplicity and letting go of excess, we contribute to a more just and sustainable world, one where resources are shared, and life's true riches can be found outside of material accumulation.

Clean Body, Clear Mind:
Living with *Shaocha*

CULTIVATING PURITY IN BODY AND MIND, or Shaocha (SHAU-chah) in Sanskrit, emphasizes both physical and mental cleanliness. Purity of body and mind underscores the importance of maintaining a clean environment and a positive mindset. Physical cleanliness entails keeping your surroundings, your home, body, and belongings orderly and hygienic. It is the foundation of a harmonious living space. It is also a sound way of maintaining health and vitality. Likewise, mental purity demands a disciplined effort to cultivate positive thoughts and to guard against negativity such as jealousy, greed, or selfishness.

Both forms of cleanliness require ongoing effort. For example, a kitchen countertop gathers dust if left unattended, necessitating regular cleaning. Similarly, our minds are prone to selfish inclinations that need constant attention and redirection. While cleaning a kitchen surface is straightforward, purifying the mind is far more challenging, often requiring consistent self-awareness and inner work.

Metta Meditation Practice

Close your eyes and take a deep breath. Let your body relax into stillness. In your mind, repeat these simple words: "May I be happy. May

I be peaceful. May I be free from suffering." At first, it may feel unusual, even uncomfortable, to direct such kindness toward yourself. Yet, notice how the words nurture a deep longing within you.

Now, recall someone you love. Picture their face clearly. Silently offer them the same blessing: "May you be happy. May you be peaceful. May you be free from suffering." Feel the warmth of these words as they flow outward from your heart toward theirs.

Next, imagine someone neutral, a neighbor you barely know, a cashier you've only seen once, or a stranger passing by on the street. Send them the same wish: "May you be happy. May you be peaceful. May you be free from suffering."

Finally, turn your attention to someone you struggle with. Perhaps a co-worker who frustrates you, a friend who hurt you, or even an adversary you've carried resentment toward for years. It may feel difficult, but offer them the same words: "May you be happy. May you be peaceful. May you be free from suffering."

This practice is called *metta* meditation, an ancient Buddhist practice of cultivating loving-kindness and sympathetic joy. It trains us to see others not as competitors or threats but as fellow beings deserving of joy and peace. The power of metta meditation lies in its simplicity. With every phrase, you train your mind to wish yourself well and others too, including those you dislike. Over time, feelings of envy, hatred, and ill will dissolve through this practice. The heart grows larger. The mind becomes pure.

Caring for People and More-Than-People

Seeing humanity as interconnected, irrespective of race, gender, class, or sexual orientation, broadens one's perspective and contributes to mental clarity. By embracing a universalist outlook, we significantly reduce selfishness and prejudice. But this outlook can extend further than human beings. We can extend our universal kindness to animals, plants, and the Earth itself, nurturing a sense of kinship with all living beings.

Baba was also the founder of Neohumanism, a philosophy which centered universalism in its worldview. Neohumanism is an innovation of humanism that moves beyond human-centered care to encompass care for more-than-human beings.[1] Baba's philosophy emphasizes the importance of transcending favoritism toward one's nation, religion, or species, advocating instead for universal love of all nations, all religions, and all beings.

Baba's book on the subject *The Liberation of Intellect: Neohumanism* (1981) offers a vast amount of knowledge that makes the case for a universalist outlook. The dedication alone at the opening of the book captures the sentiment of universalism beautifully. He writes: "To those who think for all, who offer others seats of honor and respect, who venerate others, instead of waiting to be venerated, to them I dedicate this book with humble esteem and deepest salutations."[2]

A simple technique for practicing this on a regular basis is monitoring your thoughts and replacing negative thoughts with positive thoughts. As Baba writes in *Guide to Human Conduct* (1957), "Those who are very greedy for money should form the habit of charity… Those who are angry or egoistic should cultivate the habit of being polite." These shifts in perspective not only purify the mind but also foster genuine peace of mind. Consider how transformative it can be to feel joy for a stranger's achievement or how liberating it is to let go of resentment toward someone who has wronged you.

The End of Chasing:
The Path of *Santosha*

IMAGINE SOMEONE ENJOYING a slice of their favorite cake. It fills them with delight at first. But how many slices can they eat before their senses and mind get sick of them? Eventually, the pleasure fades, and they search for another source of happiness. Yet, even if one binges on another delicious treat, the deliciousness of the new food soon comes to an end. This cycle of chasing one temporary joy after another can consume an entire lifetime without realizing it. Only when one develops a mature approach to handling desires does the search for deeper fulfillment begin.

Baba's philosophy defines happiness as the joyful feeling you get when you achieve your desires. But what happens when you don't get what you want? Is it still possible to feel happy? Maybe it's impossible to feel happy all the time, but what about contentment?

Living with contentment, or Santosha (suhn-TOH-shah) in Sanskrit, encourages us to discover joy from within rather than from external sources. It means feeling happiness whether or not we get what we want. Santosha builds on the last principle of Yama—Aparigraha, the practice of living simply and letting go of excess—by reminding us that simplicity alone is not enough. We must also cultivate genuine contentment with what we already have.

Dan Millman, in his novel, *Way of the Peaceful Warrior* (2009) writes, "The fool is happy when his cravings are satisfied. The warrior is happy for no reason." This profound idea captures the essence of true contentment: a happiness that arises not from favorable circumstances but from a deeper sense of wellness.

Consider the paradox of wealthy celebrities who, after their passing, are sometimes revealed to have lived in enormous debt. How could individuals with fame, riches, and luxury still find themselves wanting more and be drowning in debt? This speaks of an inner void that no amount of material success can fill. Living with contentment teaches us to break free from this cycle by cultivating satisfaction with what we have rather than constantly chasing more.

The Ads That Breed Discontent

In a world where we are told that satisfaction is linked to consumption, practicing Santosha is undoubtedly challenging. The marketing industry thrives on creating dissatisfaction, and marketing strategies are designed to make us feel one major thing: *I am not enough*.

With marketing pressure tapping into our insecurities all day long, we shouldn't be surprised that we cannot maintain a regular state of satisfaction. However, living with contentment reminds us we are already enough, even without the latest object or trend.

Still, contentment does not suggest passiveness in every situation. If you are being exploited, abused, or victimized, practicing Santosha would be ineffective and immoral. In such cases, dissatisfaction is not only justified but necessary for standing up for oneself. Rather, contentment applies to fostering a type of mindset that liberates us from the pull of desires that prevent us from feeling at peace with ourselves.

Living with contentment also doesn't mean settling for mediocrity or giving up on your dreams. Instead, it can remind you to find peace and joy in the journey toward your goals. Contentment allows you to appreciate where you are right now, without being consumed by the tyranny of the goal—the anxiety created around the fear of not meeting your objective.

When you practice contentment, you can work toward your aspirations with a calm and focused mind, knowing that your worth and wellness are not tied to the outcome. Ultimately, living with Santosha is about gratitude, balance, and trusting that inner contentment is far more enduring than fleeting pleasures. So, whether it's savoring a quiet moment with a cup of tea, celebrating life's little joys, or feeling gratitude for the relationships in our lives, contentment reminds us that true happiness is already within reach if we choose to embrace it.

More Than Kindness:
Understanding *Tapah*

THE MEASURE OF TRUE SERVICE is not what we give away easily, but what costs us something. If a wealthy person drops a few coins into a beggar's cup, it's a kind gesture but hardly a sacrifice. Now picture that same wealthy person helping the beggar find shelter, guiding them toward a steady job, or using their resources to create genuine opportunities. The extra effort requires time, energy, and personal investment. This is the essence of Tapah (TAH-pah)—service that is coupled with sacrifice.

Tapah is a special type of service. It may manifest through physical labor, such as assisting disaster victims by cleaning their homes or it could mean offering one's time and energy, sitting at the bedside of someone who is sick nursing them back to health. Regardless, by practicing Tapah, one develops the capacity to give to others without expectations or hidden motives.

While Tapah involves sacrifice, this sacrifice can actually feel good. Members of the yoga-affiliated Ananda Marga Universal Relief Team (AMURT) provide an interesting example. These dedicated yogi volunteers visit disaster sites, setting up refugee camps and aiding victims of natural and social upheavals. Amidst their demanding workdays, or in the late evening, they carve out moments to meditate.

During these mediations, some claim to experience a profound sense of bliss unlike any other. However, this bliss is not the yogi's main motivation. Their primary motivation is helping others by following a code of selfless service. The bliss just seems to be a pleasant side effect of their service.

Don't Over-Serve

Yet, discernment is critical in acts of selfless service. In a powerful 1864 slave narrative, Harriet Jacobs, a former enslaved woman who became an author, shares a story of misguided service.[1] Her grandmother, Martha, after enduring a lifetime of slavery, is finally freed in old age. However, Martha still maintains a friendship with her former mistress. When this former mistress asks Martha for a loan to purchase a lavish chandelier, Martha reluctantly hands over her life savings of $300, making an enormous sacrifice.

The mistress dies without repaying the debt, and her estate executors ignore Martha's claim. While Martha's loan was rooted in selflessness and friendship, it highlights the need to discern when a personal sacrifice goes too far and diminishes oneself. As Martha's experience illustrates, helping those already rich or powerful frequently has little benefit and may cause you to regret your service.

As Baba writes in *Guide to Human Conduct* (1957), "Don't waste your time flattering the rich; it will yield no result. Conquer the hearts of the underprivileged by your sympathetic behavior and accept them in your society." True service must be focused on those who genuinely need it, offering compassion, love, and effort where it can uplift the most.

Spiritual Service

Baba also spoke of service to God or the Divine. It is easy to meditate or engage in spiritual practice when life is smooth or in serene retreat settings, but true devotion shines when these acts require effort or sacrifice. For instance, skipping evening meditation to attend a party downtown may feel tempting, as pleasure is a primary motivator for human behavior. However, in moments like these, the act of meditating becomes a sacrifice. One can see the moment as an offering to the Creator instead of to oneself.

Spiritual service can also be performed when you see those you serve as expressions of the Divine. A mother nursing her child can embody this principle by seeing her infant not merely as her own but as Supreme Consciousness in the form of a child. When service is rendered with this perspective, seeing the Divine in the one being served, it transcends ordinary action and becomes a spiritual practice. It becomes Tapah.

The teaching of Tapah reminds us that service performed to gain praise, recognition, or reward loses its transformative power. Instead, we must find occasions to give fully, with no thought of receiving anything in return.

When Scripture Heals, and When it Harms: The Need for *Svadhyaya*

WHEN WE THINK OF SACRED TEXTS LIKE THE BIBLE, the Torah, or the Bhagavad Gita, we often think of them as uplifting sources of wisdom. But history also shows us the shadow side: these same texts being used to harm others.

For this reason, it is important when reading scripture to engage with it deeply to truly grasp its meaning. In Sanskrit, this practice is known as Svadhyaya (SVAHDH-yah-yah). It involves more than merely memorizing passages without comprehension. Svadhyaya invites you to enter into a dialogue with scripture, inquiring into its meaning and discerning how it applies to our lives today. When approached in this way, scripture becomes a tool for growth, healing, and transformation.

Unfortunately, people have often manipulated scriptures throughout history to justify oppression and serve selfish motives.[1] For instance, during the transatlantic slave trade, the Bible was frequently used to rationalize the enslavement of African Americans. Verses like *Ephesians 6:5*—"Slaves, obey your earthly masters with fear and trembling, with a sincere heart, as you would Christ"—were taken out of context and weaponized to endorse the institution of slavery.[2] Similarly, *Genesis 9:25—27* was cited to promote the "Curse of Ham," a misinterpretation claiming that Africans were destined for servitude. Such interpretations ignored the broader messages of love and justice within the Christian tradition, twisting scripture to serve economic and racist agendas.

The Bible has also been (and still is) used to justify the oppression of women. For example, *Timothy* 2:11–12 states, "Let a woman learn quietly with all submissiveness. I do not permit a woman to teach or to exercise authority over a man; rather, she is to remain quiet." Verses such as these have been invoked to deny women leadership roles and suppress their voices in both religious and social contexts.[3] Similarly, Genesis 3:16, which states, "Your desire shall be for your husband, and he shall rule over you," has been used to reinforce patriarchal norms and restrictive gender roles.[4]

Examples like the ones above abound in demonstrating how people have exploited religious texts for power and control, including justifying slavery, homophobia, and practices like animal sacrifice. Such distortions stem from a failure to interpret the original intent of the scriptures properly. Thus, it is crucial to approach sacred texts with discernment and to resist manipulation by those who wield scripture as a tool for personal or political gain.

Scripture has the power to either liberate or oppress, depending on how it is read and understood. As Baba mentioned in *Guide to Human Conduct* (1957), people's misinterpretations of spiritual teachings have often hindered human progress. To foster genuine spiritual growth, one must approach scripture with humility, discernment, and a commitment to truth, avoiding its misuse for personal gain. Proper understanding of scripture not only prevents harm but also helps unlock human potential for justice, compassion, and spiritual growth.

Accelerating the Soul's Journey:
The Practice of *Iishvara Pranidhana*

HOW DO YOU WANT TO WALK THE SPIRITUAL PATH? Or, if you do not consider yourself spiritual, how do you want to approach finding deeper meaning in your life? There are many different spiritual traditions that offer unique paths to deeper meaning. In Islam, for example, practices such as *salah* (five daily prayers) and *dhikr* (remembrance of God) emphasize devotion, discipline, and surrender to Allah.

The Indigenous culture of the Andes Mountains, besides prayers and contemplation, honors spiritual growth through ceremonies and kinship alliances with *Apus* (mountain guardians) to foster a deep sense of unity with *Pachamama* (the Cosmic Mother). Whether it is through prayer, meditation, ceremony, or connecting with nature, an important step in finding deeper meaning in your life is to find a practice that aligns with your heart and soul.

In Sanskrit, the practice of accelerating spiritual growth is known as Iishvara Pranidhana (EE-shvah-rah prah-NEE-dhah-nah). When you deliberately step onto a spiritual path, with dedication and focus, you are practicing this principle. It calls for seeing Source or God as the highest ideal to attain and the relationship with Source or God as the highest relationship to maintain in life.

Tantra Yoga and Mantra Meditation

One of the oldest spiritual traditions in the world is called Tantra. Westerners often confuse Tantra with a system of sexual practices. In reality, Tantra is the Indigenous spiritual tradition of India, solely focused on attaining spiritual liberation.[1] Tantra prescribes the use of a mantra for meditation practice. In Tantra, a mantra is a word or sound with deep spiritual significance. By repeating a mantra in meditation, individuals can focus their minds on the Infinite.

Through Tantric meditation, practitioners withdraw from the distractions of the external world, closing their eyes, and focusing entirely on *Brahma*, the Supreme Consciousness within. It's not enough to repeat the mantra like a parrot. One must reflect on the meaning of the mantra and connect with that intention emotionally, feeling love for the Divine. For devoted Tantric yogis, the Supreme Consciousness is the subtlest force in the universe, and She can only be attained through the depths of their devotion and feeling.

According to Baba, who was a Tantric guru, this journey toward the attainment of Brahma is not passive. It is powered by an unseen pull called *pratisainchara* (pruh-tee-suhn-chah-rah)—the natural return of all creation toward the cosmic nucleus.[2] Just as a river flows back to the ocean, all beings flow back to Source. With the help of mantra meditation, however, this return can be accelerated, allowing the meditator to move toward union with Brahma more swiftly and consciously. The mantra is the vehicle that facilitates this journey home.

Collective Spiritual Practice

When people share meditation or spiritual practice collectively, the individual bliss of each participant merges into a collective current of joy. This shared vibration often intensifies spiritual experiences, making group meditation or church services inspiring experiences. By attending collective spiritual gatherings at least once a week, one can amplify devotion, strengthen discipline, and be a part of a thriving spiritual community. The joy of shared spiritual connection fosters a sense of unity, reminding us we are not alone as we flow back toward the same divine Source.

If Tantra or mantra meditation speaks to you, consider seeking a qualified teacher to guide you. I invite you to join my online course, where I teach Tantric meditation and guide seekers on this path. Visit my website for more details at www.gustavomonje.com. The guidance of an experienced mentor can be invaluable in ensuring that you stay focused and inspired on your journey.

Finding Your Path

At this point, it is worth reflecting on what path resonates most with your spiritual needs and aspirations. You might begin by exploring your ancestral roots. What did your great-great-grandparents hold sacred, and can their wisdom still guide you today? It is also possible to learn from a tradition outside of your own culture, provided you approach it with respect, humility, and the guidance of an elder.

Weaving Together Code Two

Identifying the "Code of You"

IN THE TV DRAMA *DEXTER* (2006), originally a novel by Jim Lindsay, the protagonist is a serial killer, but not the kind you might expect. Dexter lives by a strict code: "the Code of Harry." He doesn't harm the innocent (for the most part). Those who end up under his knife are themselves other killers. In the twisted world of the show, this code makes Dexter not just tolerable, but strangely admirable. Viewers root for him because even in his darkness, he follows principles that give his actions a kind of order, even a sense of justice.

Many of us don't have that kind of clarity. We haven't defined what we truly stand for, which is why so many of us stumble, compromise, and make mistakes that pull us away from who we want to be. Without a chosen code of values, life easily gets driven by impulse, habit, or pressure from others. This chapter is your chance to change that.

Now that you've explored the Yamas and Niyamas, the ten moral principles of yoga, it's time to turn inward and define your own Core Values. The Yamas and Niyamas offer a vision of ethical living. Start by reviewing them and seeing which ones resonate with you. In case you need a reminder, here they are:

The Yamas:

- non-harming in words, thoughts, or actions (Ahimsa)
- speaking with compassion (Satya)
- non-stealing (Asteya)
- seeing everything as an expression of the divine (Brahmacharya)
- living simply (Aparigraha)

The Niyamas:

- mental and physical cleanliness (Shaocha)
- contentment (Santosha)
- selfless service (Tapah)
- spiritual study (Svadhyaya)
- accelerated spiritual growth (Iishvara Pranidhana)

Visionary Practice: Declaring Your Core Values

As you prepare to name your own values, consider dividing them into two sections: the principles that help you live in harmony with others, and the principles that help you stay in harmony with yourself.

Defining your Core Values isn't about adopting values you think you're supposed to have or clinging to ones you've inherited without question. Instead, focus on what feels most true to who you are becoming. Consider the values that will support your Higher Purpose, nurture your integrity, and provide you with inner peace.

One caution as you do this work. Resist the temptation to fill your list with values that sound like Principles of Success—words such as innovation, creativity, ambition, or excellence. These qualities belong in code four of your Higher Purpose Codex—Principles of Success.

The invitation here is different. Focus on the values that make you moral and good—the principles that ensure you live and act with compassion, integrity, and justice. Consider these guiding questions as you declare your Core Values:

- What code of conduct would I need to adopt to feel at peace with others?
- What practices should I adopt to feel at peace within myself?
- How do I want to be treated, and how should I treat others?

Step One: Brainstorming. Make a list of Core Values that are essential to how you treat others to make the world a better place. Make a list of Core Values that are essential to how you treat yourself to create peace in your mind.

Step Two: Revisiting the Higher Purpose Codex. Then, write your second code. Draft your Core Values in two categories:

Code Two
My Core Values for interacting with others are...
My Core Values for keeping peace with myself are...

Sample
My Core Values for interacting with others are speaking and acting with compassion, erasing from my mind the temptation to steal or envy what others have, treating all the way I would want to be treated, and being mindful of my consumption and ecological footprint on this Earth.

My Core Values for keeping peace with myself are keeping my mind free from criticism of myself and others, feeling gratitude for what I have, being of service to those in need to the best of my capacity, and trusting in my savior and lord Jesus Christ.

Step Three: Reflecting. Answer the following questions in your journal:

- When do I feel my Core Values are honored, and why?
- When do I feel my Core Values are being disrespected, and why?
- What changes can I make in my life to better align with my Core Values?
- How can I deepen my understanding of my Core Values?

MILESTONE MARKER. Congratulations! If you have established your Core Values and added them to your Higher Purpose Codex, you have achieved the second milestone in this book. It is a wonderful occasion to celebrate. Do something special, and share the wisdom you gained through this experience with a friend.

Part Three

Your Vision Seed

Trace Your Vision Back to Its Roots

Outside, life in the village continued as usual—people talking and children playing, but inside our small home, our world was collapsing. My brother's small, fragile body lay limp, too weak to even cry. My mother's fear was palpable, and though she tried to hide it, I could see the panic in her eyes. I could feel it in my own chest, the rising fear that something was terribly wrong. As the hours continued on, my brother's condition suddenly worsened. His body began to convulse violently, shaking uncontrollably on the floor. I stood frozen in place, unable to move as I watched him writhe in pain, his eyes wide and unfocused. My mother's cries filled the room as she tried to stop the convulsions, but nothing worked. I will never forget the hopelessness in her voice as she said, "There's nothing we can do." Her words crushed me because I knew she was right. We were powerless. We rushed him to the local nurse, but even she could do nothing. "We don't have the medicine for this," the nurse said softly, her voice heavy with sorrow.[1]

> — *Karana Conteh, How My Brother's Death*
> *Inspired My Journey into Healthcare*

THIS STORY comes from one of my former writing students Karana Conteh, originally from Sierra Leone. He writes about the heartbreaking loss of his little brother, a loss that could have been prevented with access to basic medical care. In vivid detail, Karana describes the moment when his brother's body gives out, how fear floods their small home as they realize there is nothing they can do. Through his essay, Karana shares a traumatic experience that changes the course of his life. Yet, what is most moving is the clarity of conviction that emerges from it. In a later part of his essay, Karana writes:

> Through my work in healthcare, I hope to be a source of care and hope for those who need it most, especially in communities where healthcare is not easily accessible. In the end, my brother's death was not just the end of his life; it was the beginning of my mission.[2]

That mission became his Vision Seed—becoming a nurse practitioner and serving the very communities, whose lack of resources once left his family devastated.

What is true for Karana is true for you. Your heartbreak, your grief, your longing are not absolute tragedies or screw-ups. They are the very soil in which your vision can take root. Sometimes, your mission must emerge from your deepest wounds. Like the origin stories of superheroes/sheroes, born out of pain, they are called to action. Karana's life shows you can discover a Vision Seed out of the loss of a loved one: "Every step I take is for him, and through my journey, I hope to prevent others from facing the same preventable tragedy that changed my life forever."[3]

Uncovering Your Vision Seed

Many years before I met Karana, I was asked: "What breaks your heart, and what do you want to do about it?" Ann Filemyr asked my classmates and me this question when we began her Visionary Practice and Regenerative Leadership Doctoral Program. She asked this not to guide us toward a typical research topic, but to lead us inward, to uncover our "Vision Seed"—her poetic reframe of what would traditionally be called a dissertation. Ann, an educator, poet, and spiritual guide, invited us to research with soul, not just intellect.

She showed that inside every seed is the potential for life, for beauty, for impact, but that seed cannot grow unless it breaks open. Its breaking is not a failure. It is the beginning of transformation.

By now, you've explored the deeper terrain of your Higher Purpose and named the Core Values that support your path. Now, we take the next step: moving from inner alignment to outer expression. This is where we formally introduce the concept of the Vision Seed—a purpose-driven goal that doesn't come from ambition alone but is also an expression of your Higher Purpose. It is the dream that emerges from your core, shaped by your experiences, your longings, and your desire to contribute meaningfully.

Of course, not everyone begins this process with full clarity. Some readers may still be unsure of their purpose. Others may be tempted to define their goals based on external measures of success, choosing what seems most profitable or most secure. That's understandable. Our culture often teaches us to focus on income or achievement above all else. However, the invitation here is to something different.

Goals, as we usually define them, often come from the outside in. They're shaped by timelines, expectations, and sometimes by fear. Many of us set goals because we think we "should." We pursue degrees, job titles, weight-loss targets, or financial milestones because we have been conditioned to believe that these indicate success. But many of these goals are driven more by ego, pressure, or the need for approval than by deep personal truth.

A Vision Seed is more than a goal. It is the living potential inside you to make a difference that matters. It grows out of your truth, your wounds, your wisdom, and your love. This chapter will help you name that seed and to create space for it to take root. Know that even if your Vision Seed hasn't fully revealed itself yet, you are exactly where you need to be—preparing the soil, tending the ground, and listening for what wants to emerge.

How a Vision Seed Grows

A Vision Seed is a living thing, and it needs the right conditions within you and around you to grow. Cultivating your vision is a kind of intentional gardening. You are both the soil and the gardener. The vision lives inside you, but it also depends on the quality of the ecosystem you build to support it. You don't have to do this alone.

Inner Conditions: The Soil Within

Your inner world is where the seed begins. These qualities help create fertile ground:

- **clarity:** getting honest about what matters to you and what you're ready to grow
- **willingness:** being open to the process, even if you don't feel completely "ready"
- **self-reflection:** making time to listen inwardly, to ask, discern, and adjust
- **emotional honesty:** allowing yourself to feel fear, excitement, grief, or hope without shame
- **intuitive guidance:** trusting and feeling that the Universe is guiding your way and everything around you

Despite these important prerequisites, you don't need to be perfect to start. But you need to tend to yourself like good soil and become soft enough to let something in, rich enough to support growth, and open enough to let the light through.

Outer Conditions: Building Your Support Ecosystem

No one grows a Vision Seed alone. One of the most loving things you can do for your Vision Seed is to create an outer environment that nourishes it. Create a small group of people who can support your vision's growth. This might include:

- a trusted friend who listens deeply and encourages you without judgment
- a colleague or collaborator who helps you execute the technical aspects of your project
- a mentor or guide who has experience in the area your vision touches
- a coach, therapist, or spiritual elder who can help you stay grounded and clear
- a peer or a community who are also pursuing a similar vision to yours and can walk beside you

Choose people who are not just skilled but aligned. You want people who believe in what you're growing and who won't sabotage your dreams—people who share your Core Values or deeply respect them.

Make Peace With Where You Are Now

There is no one right way for a vision to look, and no single timeline for it to unfold. Some Vision Seeds blossom quickly, taking the form of a new project, healing practice, business, or creative offering. Others grow slowly, overcoming the Survival State, requiring healing, or beginning a deep inner shift that won't be visible to anyone else for a long time. Some people are ready to pour time and energy into their vision now. Others may be physically unable to start. For now, just holding your seed close is important, while getting through an enormous challenge one day at a time.

Some days, I think about my grandfather, Juan Jose, who even in his old age would still dream despite his limitations. He spent his last years writing a script for a TV show about drug addiction. He also had a big desire to teach public speaking to his peers in retirement homes. These dreams didn't fully materialize in his lifetime, but they came from his heart, and they inspired me a great deal.

Maybe you're reading this while staying at a women's shelter. Or maybe you're sleeping in a friend's basement, unsure of what comes next. You might be juggling two jobs, raising children on your own, or navigating a health crisis. Your primary concern right now may be putting food on the table or finding a moment of peace in the middle of a storm. Or maybe you are just exhausted from your regular routine. All of this is okay.

A Vision Seed that stems from your Higher Purpose remains alive inside your heart, where hope lives. Some visions take the long road. Some need time to get clear. Life has many seasons. Some seasons are meant for healing, for rest, or for survival—not for building something big. The Bible says, "To everything there is a season, a time for every purpose under heaven... a time to break down, and a time to build up; a time to weep, and a time to laugh; a time to mourn, and a time to dance."[4] Living with purpose means finding purpose in all the seasons of your life and holding your vision close.

But what if planting your Vision Seed requires more education, credentials, financial support, or mental clarity before you can fully begin? That's normal, too. Before planting your Vision Seed, you may feel the need to enroll in a class or certificate program. Or maybe you need to create a more stable living situation, get support for mental health or trauma healing, save money, or seek a grant. Finally, maybe you need to find a mentor or trusted elder to settle important questions. These feelings are valid.

These actions may be the first steps in planting your Vision Seed. They are foundations, not detours. Every effort you make to care for yourself, strengthen your skill set, or create supportive conditions is a way of saying yes to your vision, even if it won't get to the outcome right away.

Here are some practical ways to plant your seed, even if you're not ready to nurture it fully:

- **write it down:** Keep a small notebook or notes app where you capture ideas, dreams, and longings.
- **name it to someone you trust:** Saying it out loud gives it shape.
- **start a Vision Seed folder:** Collect articles, images, quotes, or resources that speak to your future path.
- **make micro-moves:** Choose one small, doable action that keeps your seed alive each week— even 10 minutes of brainstorming counts.
- **honor this season:** If now is a time for survival or healing, do that. Your Vision Seed needs you well and whole.

Starting Now

For those who are in a season where the seed can be planted—where the energy, support, and clarity have aligned—know this: the time is now. You don't have to wait for the perfect moment. Starting, even with trembling hands and limited tools, allows you to forge a path ahead, step by step.

In the next chapter, you'll enter a reflective space and complete a survey to help you explore potential Vision Seeds in multiple areas: career, creativity, relationships, spirituality, community, or healing. As you work through the exercise, give yourself permission to dream regardless of where you are right now in your life.

Visionary Practice: Holding Space for Your Vision Seed

This week, set the intention for clarity on your Vision Seed. Ask the Universe to help you create alignment between your Higher Purpose, Core Values, and Vision Seed.

Create a vision board illustrating how you want your Vision Seed to manifest. Get clear. Make it an offering to the Universe of what you hope to create in the world. A vision board is a visual tool that helps you clarify and focus on what matters most. It is created by collecting images, words, or symbols and then arranging them on a poster board, journal page, or digital canvas. To make one, reflect on your Vision Seed, then gather pictures from magazines or online sources, along with meaningful words or affirmations. Arrange them in a way that inspires you, creating a visual representation of what you are calling into being.

What Will You Grow?

IMAGINE YOUR LIFE AS A GARDEN. Some plants in this garden were already here before you arrived—your family, your culture, and the society you were born into. Others were planted later, like your schooling, your job, and other responsibilities. All the plants and trees in this garden need tending. Some plants you water with joy. Others you tend out of duty or expectation. It may appear there is no more room in this garden to plant anything new. Other times, it may feel as if you will forever be busy tending the same plants you've long cared for, whether out of sentiment or obligation.

Wait! What if there were room? What new seeds would you plant? What fruit would you like to harvest from the plants already under your care? And what visions, still hidden in your heart, might be ready to take root if you gave them space?

This chapter is your opportunity to explore those questions and acknowledge what you want to grow. Imagine all your goals and aspirations as plants that need nurturing to grow. Ask yourself: *What fruits do I hope to receive from my "physical wellness plant" or my "professional career plant?"*

Some areas of life may feel clear, and you know exactly what you hope to grow from them. Others may feel uncertain because you have hardly given them attention. You don't need to have everything figured out perfectly. Simply allow yourself the space to dream.

Visionary Practice: Vision Seeds Survey

Through this survey, you will identify your Vision Seeds in 12 different areas of life. You will reflect on the conditions they need to grow, and rate how important they are at this time. You'll close the survey by identifying your top Vision Seeds. Let the answers to your survey be a sacred inventory of what is ready to grow. Here are the categories you will examine:

Physical Wellness

Examples: recovering from a disease, improving diet, establishing a consistent exercise routine

Emotional Wellness

Examples: managing anxiety or depression, recovering from trauma

Spiritual Wellness

Examples: deepening a connection with God, Mother Earth, or the Universe

Education

Examples: completing a college degree, getting a certification in Professional Writing

Professional and Career Aspirations

Examples: becoming an IT professional, a published author, or a personal trainer

Financial Wellness

Examples: acquiring financial stability or increasing income and improving personal budgeting skills

Intellectual Growth and Interests

Examples: learning a new skill, such as marketing or coding

Social Life and Relationships

Examples: improving social skills, finding a life partner, repairing ruptured family relationships

Connection to Nature and More-Than-Human Beings

Examples: planting a garden, adopting a pet, or hiking more trails.

Advocacy and Causes

Examples: supporting social movements like Black Lives Matter or anti-war campaigns

Personal Routine and Organization

Examples: developing a weekly schedule, time blocking, or creating a consistent morning routine

Creative Projects

Examples: recording an album of music or learning photography

Take a Moment to Ground Yourself

If this feels right to you, pause before beginning and ask a Higher Power, Source, or any aspect of Spirit that resonates with you to assist you in this exercise. Ask for this Visionary Practice to be a successful undertaking that will lead you to uncover your Vision Seed.

Guidelines

Answer the questions below for each of the categories above in your journal:

- Category (physical wellness, financial wellness):
- My Vision Seed for this category is:

- This aligns with my Higher Purpose or my Core Values in the following way:
- Importance Rating (1-5):
- What kind of environment does this Vision Seed need to grow? What might it look like when it blooms?

Reflection

Identify Your Top Three Vision Seeds. After considering all the categories, what are the top three Vision Seeds you want to focus on? Pay attention to the categories that were rated higher in importance.

Identify the Intersection of Vision Seeds. Do any of your Vision Seeds connect across multiple categories? If yes, what is the connection?

Deeper Reflection. Write a paragraph about one or all of the Vision Seeds you selected, stating why these areas are of most importance to you.

In case you would like to fill this survey out digitally, you scan the QR code below to access a document with each category followed by the questions:

Planting Your Vision Seed

"Your vision will become clear only when you can look into your own heart."

— *Carl Jung, Letters, Volume 2: 1951-1961*

BY NOW, YOU'VE BEEN LISTENING DEEPLY to your Higher Purpose, to the Core Values that mark your integrity, and to how these might take shape as Vision Seeds in the form of your work and actions. You've been preparing the soil.

Now, you'll take the next step in expanding your Higher Purpose Codex by naming your Vision Seed(s). Remember, this isn't just about achievement. It's about alignment. You're not just choosing a goal because it sounds good. You're naming something that reflects your values, your wisdom, and the unique gifts you bring to the world. As my mentor Ann Filemyr teaches, a Vision Seed is a spark of an idea or a personal calling. This chapter invites you to take the first steps in nurturing, incubating, and bringing that life-giving spark into form so it may fulfill your unique purpose.

Don't worry about not getting this perfect. You're not making a final decision for the rest of your life. You're simply listening to what feels most alive right now and honoring it by writing it down.

Visionary Practice: Planting Your Vision Seed

Step One: Brainstorming. At this moment in your life, what is the biggest dream stemming from your unique purpose that wants to come into the world? If you have more than one, that is okay. You can list multiple Vision Seeds.

Step Two: Revisit the Higher Purpose Codex. Then, write your third code.

Code Three
To bring my Higher Purpose to action, I am planting the following Vision Seed(s)...

Sample
To bring my Higher Purpose to action, I am planting the following Vision Seed: I will launch a podcast that amplifies Indigenous voices fighting for sovereignty across the Americas.

Step Three: Reflecting. Answer the following questions to gain deeper clarity and insight:

- Does your Vision Seed align with your Higher Purpose?
- How does it support and contribute to that purpose? If it doesn't, what steps can you take to bridge the gap?
- How do your Core Values enhance, protect, or strengthen your Vision Seed? For example, if one of your values is showing kindness to all, how can this assist you in a Vision Seed related to becoming a nurse practitioner?
- Why is this Vision Seed meaningful to you?
- What steps can you take now to fulfill your Vision Seed?

Step Four: Engage with Others for Feedback. This week, share your Vision Seed with at least three people (mentors, family members, friends, or colleagues) and ask for their feedback. Encourage them to offer new ideas, fresh perspectives, or actionable advice to help nurture and clarify your goal. After these conversations, reflect on the following:

- What feedback did you receive?
- Did any new insights or leads emerge?
- Has your Vision Seed become more specific or focused based on the input you received?

Allow the process of reflection and feedback to sharpen your focus and fuel your journey.

MILESTONE MARKER. Congratulations! If you have successfully written your Vision Seed statement and extended your Higher Purpose Codex, you have accomplished the third milestone in our book. This is a cause for celebration! Treat yourself to something special.

Part Four

Your Principles of Success

Learn the "Seven" Secrets of Success

AROUND SEVEN THOUSAND YEARS AGO, in ancient India, lived a guru named Sadashiva, known simply across time as Shiva. He lived with his wife Parvatii. They were not only husband and wife but also teacher and disciple. Shiva was regarded as a source of spiritual knowledge—the first to systematize practices of yoga and meditation in ways that ordinary people could understand.[1] Parvatii, played a vital role in these teachings. She was highly intellectual and spiritually developed. In their conversations, she voiced the questions of humanity: the doubts, longings, and confusions of seekers everywhere.

In one of these dialogues, Parvatii asked, "Shiva, everyone is looking for success in life. What are the secrets to success?"[2] Shiva's response was practical. He answered, "There are seven secrets to success." These secrets provide a comprehensive pathway to success not just in spiritual life, but for all aspects that are valued in modern life. The answers can help you in business, education, goal setting or in any area where you may seek success.

According to Baba, these sacred conversations between Parvatii and Shiva became the very foundation of the Tantric scriptures. Parvatii's sincere questions formed the *Nigama*—the philosophical and theoretical inquiries of Tantra. Shiva's answers became the *Agama*—

the practical instructions for how to live and practice. Together, these formed the Tantra *Shastra*, a body of wisdom that has guided seekers for millennia.[3] Through Parvatii and Shiva's timeless exchange, we glimpse an essential part of Tantra: a dialogue between the eternal question of the human heart and the guidance of Divine wisdom.

Before you can fully grow your Vision Seed, you need to learn how to take care of it. A vision is powerful—but without the right mindset, disciplines, tools, and habits, it can fade or fall apart. That's why in the next chapters you will examine "seven" principles of success that can assist you in gaining what you seek. Some of them are taught just as Baba explained them from Shiva's teachings, and some are gently adapted so they're easier to apply to a larger audience. You'll reflect on what success truly means and how the "seven" secrets can support your Vision Seed. Are you wondering why seven is written in quotation marks? You'll have to read further to learn. At the end of this section, you'll choose Principles of Success that feel most important to you. These will become the next code in your Higher Purpose Codex.

Visionary Practice: Holding Space for Your Principles of Success

This week, reflect on the power of sacred questions and sacred answers. Return to the teachings of Nigama (Parvatii's questions) and Agama (Shiva's responses). On a small piece of paper, write a question such as: *What is the meaning of success?* or *How can I be successful in my Vision Seed?*

Place the paper under your pillow before you sleep, and ask the Universe to bring the answer to you in a dream. Keep a pen or pencil nearby so you can capture whatever comes through. If you wake up the next morning without an answer, simply continue the practice.

Keep the question under your pillow and your pen within reach. Trust that the answer will arrive in its own time.

When the message appears, you will recognize it. The Divine has a way of making dreams unmistakably clear to give you the answer. Sometimes, the guidance arrives all at once; other times, it comes in small pieces across several dreams. Stay open, attentive, and trusting of your intuition.

Firm Determination: Bridging Skill and Achievement

NOW THAT YOU HAVE PLANTED YOUR VISION SEED, you need to be consistent in watering it and monitoring its growth. You will need firm determination—the power to set your mind on a goal and keep moving toward it with consistency and enthusiasm, no matter the obstacles. With each intentional thought and action, determination draws you closer to your goal. It is the quality that can make or break your journey. However, developing firm determination does not always come easily.

Three Approaches to Effort

The Non-Starter. Giselle dreamed of running her first marathon. She researched training plans, bought the perfect running shoes, and imagined herself crossing the finish line. But as she remembered her failed fitness attempts in the past, doubt crept in. *What if I fail again?* Fear paralyzed her. The shoes remained untouched, and her Vision Seed withered before it could sprout.

The Quitter. Josue was determined to tone his body at the gym. He signed up excited and completed his first few sessions. Alongside his workouts, he began a new diet regimen, determined to follow it strictly. But after a few days, he slipped, grabbing fast food on a stressful night and skipping meals on another. These minor setbacks discouraged him. *I've already ruined my progress,* he thought. Feeling thrown off his plan, Josue spiraled into self-doubt. When his weight didn't change after a couple of weeks, the discouragement deepened. *I'll never catch up to everyone else,* he told himself. Frustrated and disheartened, Josue stopped going to the gym altogether, overwhelmed by comparisons and his perceived inadequacies.

The Achiever. Mia set her sights on finishing her degree while working part-time and being a single mother. The journey had many obstacles: late nights after putting her kids to bed and long days balancing work. Like Josue, she also stumbled along the way. Some nights she was too exhausted to complete her assignments, and there were moments she doubted whether she could juggle it all. But unlike Josue, she didn't let her setbacks define her. When she slipped, she adjusted. She asked family for help, sought extensions when necessary, and carved out quiet moments to study whenever she could. For Mia, each challenge became a stepping-stone. In time, she walked across the stage to receive her diploma, her Vision Seed fully realized.

These three stories show different approaches to effort. Giselle never began. Josue started but quit too soon. Mia persevered and succeeded because she showed firm determination. Her story shows the best approach to accomplishing your Vision Seed.

The Power of Grit

We often believe that talent is the key to success, assuming that extraordinary individuals must be born with some magical gift. Whether it's an entertainer like Beyoncé or a basketball legend like LeBron James, we romanticize their abilities as if they were born fully formed.

Yet, the reality is different. Their greatness is the result of countless hours of practice, relentless perseverance, and gradual improvement.

In her 2016 book, *Grit: The Power of Passion and Perseverance,* psychologist Angela Duckworth explains how grit often predicts success better than talent or IQ. Her studies, conducted in competitive environments like West Point Academy and the Scripps National Spelling Bee, reveal that candidates with the most grit, not the most talent, prevail. In fact, Angela Duckworth has developed a "grit formula," which equates the following: "Talent x Effort = Skill. Skill x Effort = Achievement."[1]

This means consistent effort is the multiplier that transforms potential into success. Even if you don't feel "talented," effort and practice can help you gain a new skill. Then developing your skill with continued effort allows you to achieve extraordinary results. Albert Einstein, often hailed as a genius, famously attributed his success to "1% talent and 99% hard work.[2] Einstein was a living example of how the myth of talent often blinds us to the truth: effort and persistence are the real magic behind extraordinary achievements.

Consistent Effort vs Overthinking

In his book *Atomic Habits* (2018), James Clear recounts a story about Jerry Uelsmann, a photography professor at the University of Florida. Uelsmann divided his class into two groups. The first group, the "Quantity Group," was tasked with taking as many photos as possible during the semester, while the second group, the "Quality Group," was told to focus on creating one perfect photo. Which of the two groups do you think took the best photos?

By the end of the semester, the best photos came from the Quantity Group. Their consistent effort, taking photo after photo, enabled them to learn from their mistakes and improve over time. In contrast, the Quality Group spent so much time overthinking that they failed to achieve the same level of mastery. This example demonstrates the grit formula in action: repeated effort builds skill, and skill multiplied by effort leads to achievement. By embracing consistent action, you can transform potential into extraordinary outcomes.

The 10,000-Hour Rule

The book *Outliers* (2011) by Malcolm Gladwell explores what separates exceptional performers from the rest. One of Gladwell's key findings is the "10,000-Hour Rule," which suggests that to achieve world-class expertise in any field, a person tends to invest at least 10,000 hours of deliberate practice. The "10,000-Hour Rule" aligns closely with the grit formula: talent may set the stage, but it is consistent effort over time that refines skill and leads to achievement. It's a reminder that mastery is not about innate ability but about dedicating the time and effort needed to reach the top.

Gladwell draws on examples like The Beatles, who played live shows in Hamburg, Germany, over 1,200 times before they rose to global fame. This intense practice, totaling well over 10,000 hours, honed their skills and prepared them for success. It's not like they played in perfect conditions or for very large audiences. Yet, through commitment and perseverance, their dreams of stardom came true. Another example is the late basketball legend Kobe Bryant, who was known for his relentless work ethic.[3] Bryant famously began training at 4 a.m., dedicating countless hours to perfecting his skill. His commitment to deliberate practice made him one of the greatest athletes in history.

What is something that you can see yourself doing for about 10,000 hours? Consider your Vision Seed—do you see yourself working on it for 10,000 hours? Does your Vision Seed even require 10,000 hours of dedication, or can it be accomplished with much less time? It may be a good idea to nurture a Vision Seed that you feel you could devote 10,000 hours to passionately. This way, you may never fall short of motivation. However, I don't want to scare you. Your Vision Seed or your areas of growth may not need 10,000 hours. However long it takes, the point is to embrace consistent effort.

Embracing Obstacles

Obstacles are inevitable in life and on the path to success. In fact, the bigger the goal, the bigger the obstacles. Every genius has their story of struggle. In a discourse from 1978, Baba said of obstacles:

> The more vigorously one tries to move towards the goal, the more vehemently one will have to fight against obstacles. Those who are averse to struggle will never make any progress; what to speak of progress without struggle, one will lag behind. Hence, struggle is the essence of life.[4]

To face struggle, Baba encouraged his followers to befriend their obstacles. Obstacles should not be seen as roadblocks but as helping forces that push us closer to our goals. When approached with a growth mindset, obstacles can serve as stepping-stones to success. Each challenge we face provides an opportunity to practice firm determination, build resilience, and strengthen our resolve.

Think about your early development. You learned to crawl, walk, and talk. None of this was easy. All of this growth came with obstacles. You cried because you didn't have the vocabulary to express yourself. Other times, you cried because you tripped and fell. Consider how these trials and clashes gave rise to new possibilities. Baba emphasized, "The struggle to overcome obstacles is the primary factor in the development of the mind."[5] Here are some strategies to befriend your obstacles:

Reframe Your Perspective. View obstacles as opportunities for growth rather than barriers. Ask yourself, "What can I learn from this challenge? How can this make me stronger?"

Practice Gratitude. Instead of resisting obstacles, practice gratitude for the lessons they bring. Every challenge can teach you patience, creativity, or perseverance.

Break Down Challenges. Large obstacles can feel overwhelming. Break them into smaller, manageable steps, and tackle each one methodically. Celebrate small victories along the way.

Develop a Resilient Mindset. Cultivate mental adaptability by visualizing success even in the face of difficulty. Remind yourself of past challenges you've overcome. Use them to view your journey differently and as proof of your capabilities.

Seek Support. Obstacles are easier to navigate with the help of a supportive ecosystem. Share your struggles with friends, mentors, or spiritual guides who can provide encouragement and perspective.

By befriending obstacles and embracing them as helpful parts of your journey, you transform them into allies. Try invoking the spirit of one of my favorite animal guides, the ram. The ram offers a metaphor for overcoming challenges. With his elegant horns, the ram charges head-on, breaking through barriers.

Setting Goals

Setting and pursuing goals can be transformative, especially when approached with structure and accountability. Research by Dr. Gail Matthews at Dominican University found that people who wrote down their goals and shared weekly updates with a friend were more than twice as likely to succeed as those who kept their goals to themselves—76% success compared to only 35%.[6] Her findings highlight three powerful practices:

- **write it down:** Putting your goals in writing makes them clear and concrete.
- **make a plan:** Break goals into small, specific steps that are actionable.

- **stay accountable:** Share your goals with someone you trust and send regular updates to stay consistent.

The takeaway is simple: your Vision Seed is far more likely to grow when you write it down, plan it out, and invite others to support you. Success doesn't rely on willpower alone. It flourishes through intention, structure, and accountability. Find an accountability partner, write your goals down, and revisit them often. It's a small habit that can make a powerful difference.

Whether you're striving to master a skill, overcome obstacles, or achieve your Vision Seed, remember this: persistence transforms potential into achievement. Start now, take small steps daily, and embrace the journey. Let your grit carry you forward toward fulfilling your Vision Seed. The road to success is paved with perseverance, not perfection. Every great achievement starts with a simple commitment: to show up, to keep going, and to trust in the process.

Pursuing Universal Truth:
Trading Glitter for Gold

"Where are you? Here.

What time is it? Now.

What are you? This moment."

— Dan Millman, Way of the Peaceful
Warrior: A Book That Changes Lives

IMAGINE SOMEONE ASKING, "WHAT TIME IS IT?" You glance at your watch and answer, "It's 3:30 PM." But is it 3:30 PM everywhere? In Tokyo, it could be 7:30 AM the next day. In New Mexico, it might only be 1:30 PM. Even as we speak, the seconds are ticking by, making the original answer obsolete. Time is a prime example of relativity. It depends on where you are and when you're asking. It's always changing. Much of life mirrors this dynamic. Many aspects of our existence are context-dependent and constantly shifting. These are what we call relative truths.

Consider life's ups and downs. Today's struggles may feel overwhelming, yet a decade from now, they could be the foundation of your greatest growth. Similarly, relationships evolve. Someone who is central to your life today may have been a stranger before and could become one again if you drift apart. Even our ambitions shift. A goal that feels essential now may lose its meaning as we grow.

Similarly, your current Vision Seed may feel like an absolute guiding star. But it is essential to acknowledge its transient nature in the broader journey of life. Understanding that these truths are fluid helps us navigate life with greater ease, appreciating the present without becoming overly attached to what will inevitably change.

Yet recognizing that so much of life is relative invites an important question: where can we find stability? If truth and circumstances are constantly shifting, then what anchors us? One way to approach this is by examining the values that guide our lives, distinguishing between those that are fleeting and those that endure. These values that endure are our universal truths.

Extrinsic and Intrinsic Values

Johann Hari, in his book *Lost Connections* (2018), sought to uncover the true causes of anxiety and depression. Among his findings, he identified nine major causes of anxiety and depression, one of which was the over-reliance on extrinsic values.[1] Extrinsic values are things we appreciate because of what they can provide, such as status, wealth, or approval. Hari describes money as a classic example.

Imagine receiving a suitcase filled with a million dollars. At first, excitement surges through you. But what if you're told you can never spend it? Suddenly, the bills become meaningless paper. Like money, many of the things we chase—job titles, social status, or material possessions—hold value only because of what they promise. When we place too much importance on extrinsic values, we risk tying our happiness to things that are fleeting and beyond our control.

What are intrinsic values? Intrinsic values, on the other hand, are meaningful in and of themselves. Spirituality can be an example of an intrinsic value. When you engage in spiritual practices out of love or connection, the experience itself is fulfilling, regardless of any external reward. However, if spirituality becomes a transactional act (praying to "earn" blessings or a spot in heaven), it shifts from an intrinsic pursuit to an extrinsic one. Intrinsic values can provide sustained happiness because they nourish you directly, offering a sense of meaning, purpose, and fulfillment that does not depend on outside validation or reward.

In the 1980s, Tim Kasser, a professor, psychologist, author and researcher, conducted a study on two key drivers of human behavior: intrinsic and extrinsic motives.[2] His findings validated conventional wisdom that doing what you love makes you happier. An LA Times newspaper article illustrated intrinsic and extrinsic motives in the following way:

> Imagine you play the piano. If you play it in the morning because it gives you joy, that is an intrinsic motive—you aren't doing it to get anything else out of it; you are doing it simply because that experience is worth doing, in and of itself. Now imagine you play the piano to impress your parents, or in a dive bar you hate to pay the rent, or to seduce somebody into sleeping with you. That would be an extrinsic motive—you aren't doing it because you think the experience is worthwhile; you are doing it to get something out of it.[3]

Kasser's studies showed that people with extrinsic orientations reported worse physical and mental health.[4] They felt sicker, angrier, and less joyful. Their relationships suffered, and they experienced greater insecurity. Kasser concluded that achieving extrinsic goals, like a promotion, a fancy car, or the newest iPhone, did not increase day-to-day happiness. These accomplishments provided no lasting joy.

In stark contrast, people who pursued intrinsic goals experienced significant improvements in happiness and reductions in anxiety and depression. For example, becoming a better friend or parent, dancing simply for the joy of it, joining a volunteer group, rising early to meditate, or helping family members because it felt right led to deeper satisfaction with life.[5]

Choosing Career Paths

Over the years, as a community college English professor, I tried using different themes in my writing courses to engage students. I tried implementing themes on global warming or government surveillance. To my dismay, none seemed to resonate deeply. That changed when I introduced the theme of "Planting Your Vision Seed" and explored how a college writing course could be tied to purpose setting and life coaching. The new theme created more intrinsic value, which the students appreciated. It has become a powerful way to help them gain self-knowledge and become more reflective writers.

For most of my students, the Vision Seeds they name in class are closely tied to their degree plans. Their writing often reveals that their career paths are primarily motivated by economic gain. To show the challenges of choosing careers with extrinsic motives, I share my experience with them.

Neither of my parents graduated from college. When I arrived at the dorms at Antioch College, where I got my bachelor's degree, I felt a deep sense of imposter syndrome. Seeing my name on the door of my dorm and realizing the college actually expected me to live there as a student was surreal. The pressure to succeed during my first semester led me to choose pre-med as a major, thinking I should pursue a "real" career, to make college worthwhile.

Not surprisingly, I failed chemistry and realized the hard sciences weren't for me. "Everyone has a plan until they get punched in the face," is a wise quote usually attributed to Mike Tyson, and I felt what he meant. In my story, I try to show that sometimes students struggle academically, not because they lack intellectual ability, but because they are studying subjects they don't genuinely enjoy.

While I failed chemistry my first semester, my college experience was opening my eyes to new knowledge I genuinely enjoyed about society, race, class, and gender. I wondered why in high school I never studied these themes. These revelations inspired me to become a teacher, driven by the joy I would feel, empowering young people to think critically about society, especially those who were outside the status quo. I was right. I love teaching because I don't see education as filling people with information, but as gently tending a flame, helping something already alive inside a person grow brighter and more confident. Thanks to pursuing a career aligned with intrinsic values, I have spent the last 20 years of my life as an educator, and I have never regretted it once.

The Allure and Danger of "Junk Values"

Junk food can sometimes count as a meal, but it fails to meet our nutritional needs. In much the same way, "junk values" promise fulfillment but leave our deeper psychological needs, for connection and meaning, starving. As Johann Hari (2018) aptly puts it, "Extrinsic values are KFC for the soul." However, in a culture driven by consumerism, people are relentlessly pushed to live extrinsically, chasing shallow rewards at the expense of what truly matters.

This manipulation starts young. In *Lost Connections* (2018), Hari highlights a 1978 Canadian study measuring the impact of advertisements on children. Over a two-week period, four- and five-year-olds were divided into two groups. One group watched no commercials, while the other group saw just two ads for a toy. Afterward, the children were given a choice: they could play with the toy, but the catch was that the toy belonged to a mean-spirited boy they'd have to play with to get it. Alternatively, they could forgo the toy and play with a friendly boy instead.

The results Hari describes are striking. The children who hadn't seen the commercials overwhelmingly chose to play with the friendly boy, ignoring the toy. In contrast, the children exposed to the ads prioritized the toy, even at the cost of interacting with an unpleasant playmate. Just two commercials were enough to make them value a piece of plastic over meaningful social interaction.

If such a brief exposure to advertising can sway the values of children, consider the effect of the 4,000 to 10,000 ads the average US citizen is exposed to daily.[6] Billboards flash by as we drive, logos cover our clothes, and screens bombard us with messages designed to make us crave things we don't need. I still remember the jarring moment when product advertisements started appearing before films at the movie theater. What once was a space reserved for previews of upcoming films became another avenue for Coca-Cola and local businesses to compete for our attention.

These omnipresent ads are not just noise. They craft a powerful narrative about who we are and what we lack. The essence of this narrative, shaped by capitalism, is simple: You are not enough. There is always someone more attractive, more successful, more deserving. There is always a product promising happiness, a gadget to make life easier, a cream to make you more beautiful, a new car to make you feel accomplished. Oh, and if you don't have it, you're falling behind. The more ads erode our self-esteem, the more likely we are to buy into their promises of convenience and prosperity. It's no wonder companies pour billions of dollars into advertising: it works. They're getting richer. If they weren't, they wouldn't keep doing it.[7]

What's truly alarming is how this constant exposure shapes our cultural values, shifting our focus from what genuinely matters—connection, creativity, and purpose. We trade meaningful pursuits for the fleeting satisfaction of acquiring something new, yet as we accumulate more, we feel less fulfilled, trapped in a cycle of wanting and consuming.

Breaking free requires a conscious effort to challenge this narrative by asking ourselves hard questions: *Are our goals shaped by what we truly value, or by what we've been told to value? Are we pursuing connection and purpose, or simply reacting to a culture that thrives on our insecurities?* By recognizing the influence of junk values, we can begin to reclaim our agency and refocus on what brings genuine joy and meaning to our lives.

Shraddha: Having Devotion for Universal Truth

Neither our bodies nor our minds represents universal truth. For example, our bodies change: they grow, age, and eventually deteriorate. Even what we think, and how we see things changes. But what about our spiritual side? Beneath the layers of our physical and mental existence lies a simple, enduring life force: consciousness, the part of us that allows us to be self-aware. Our consciousness is a universal truth. It remains constant throughout the transformations of our bodies and minds.

Is there anything you know for certain? Perhaps the only thing you know for certain is that you exist. Your awareness of yourself is proof of consciousness. When you observe the world, plants, animals, people, and even inanimate objects you see countless forms. Yet, in each form, one thing is certain: they are expressions of life, Spirit, or consciousness, depending on your preferred terminology. The recognition of consciousness existing within everything is also an example of a universal truth.

Consciousness is the unifying thread that connects all aspects of the universe. It is not the abstract nothingness of the universe. It is the source of everything. Taking the time to connect with the infinite realm of consciousness allows us to tap into a boundless source of wisdom and love. Understanding consciousness is at the heart of pursuing universal truth.

Baba inspired his followers to practice *shraddha*—having deep reverence and devotion for Supreme Consciousness. Shraddha is about cultivating a heartfelt connection with the Divine. Surveys by the Pew Research Center and other global studies find that large majorities of people in most countries report belief in God or some spiritual force, illustrating how widespread belief in a higher power remains worldwide.[8] However, how many of those individuals truly have a personal relationship with that Supreme Entity?

For many, the concept of God remains abstract. It's easy to say logically, "There must be a God, because everything has to come from somewhere." But what do we do with that realization? How does it shape our daily lives? Without a meaningful connection, the Supreme often feels distant, vague, and difficult to relate to. Just as we seek fulfillment through intrinsic values, the deepest fulfillment comes from aligning with the ultimate intrinsic value—our connection to the creator of all.

To develop shraddha or reverence, it helps to personalize our relationship with the creator. Consider how various religious traditions approach this. For instance, Christians often refer to God as a Father. Phrases like "The Father and the Son" create a familial connection that makes the Divine relatable. By viewing God as a loving father, one can adopt the role of a devoted child, fostering a sense of intimacy and devotion.

However, devotion can wane, especially when hardship arises in life. It's difficult to reconcile the idea of a loving Supreme Consciousness with the existence of pain, injustice, and loss. When prayers seem unanswered or hardships persist, doubt can creep in, making the Supreme feel distant or indifferent.

Yet, suffering is not evidence of abandonment but a call to deepen our understanding. Just as darkness makes light more visible, challenges can illuminate the strength of our inner connection to the Divine. Try not to ask yourself questions like, *Why does God allow this?* Instead, consider: *How can this experience shape me into someone wiser, stronger, and more compassionate?*

Shifting our focus from blaming the Divine to seeking deeper understanding allows us to transform suffering into growth. Just as fire tempers metal, struggles refine our character, making us more resilient and attuned to seeking refuge in something greater than ourselves. True devotion is not about expecting a life free from hardship but about recognizing that our struggles have purpose, and we are never alone as we navigate them. By embracing daily spiritual practices such as prayer, meditation, or acts of service, we create a consistent connection to the Infinite, one that sustains us through every storm.

Here are some methods to deepen your connection with Supreme Consciousness:

Establish a Personal Relationship. Visualize the Divine as a loving guide—a Father, Mother, or close Friend, who supports you in all circumstances.

Seek Inspiration From Spiritual Masters. Learn from those who have embodied Supreme Consciousness, allowing their wisdom to guide your journey.

Engage in Daily Practices. Strengthen your connection through daily prayer, meditation, or ceremony. Imagine yourself held in the embrace of Divine love.

See the Divine in Everything. Recognize that Supreme Consciousness pervades all aspects of existence, such as nature, people, and even the smallest moments of daily life.

Pursuing universal truth means aligning with what is timeless and deeply meaningful. Connecting to the greater consciousness that unites all things leads to more than happiness. It leads to bliss.

Finding the Right Guide: Choosing Teachers Who Uplift

IT WAS THE FULL MOON OF AUGUST IN 1939. Kalicharan, a feared criminal in Calcutta known for his ruthlessness, prowled the edge of a cremation ground by the Hooghly River, waiting for nightfall to carry out his crimes. But that night, he spotted an unusual figure. By the riverbank, bathed in the moonlight, sat an 18-year-old Baba, my guru, completely motionless, exuding an aura of calm and wisdom. Kalicharan, however, didn't see any of those qualities. All he saw were pockets and wondered how much money he might find on this young man to steal.

Kalicharan made sure the area was deserted. He crouched like a predator, inching closer with a knife in hand, ready to pounce on his target. But just as he prepared to strike, Baba, without turning his head, spoke Kalicharan's name in a voice both commanding and gentle, "Kalicharan, is that you? Come, take a seat."

Startled, Kalicharan froze. *Who's playing tricks on me?* he thought to himself. But the voice had a strange power that compelled him to obey. He lowered his weapon and sat down, confused. "How do you know my name?" Kalicharan demanded. The young guru softened his face and began to recount intimate details of Kalicharan's past: the streets he haunted, the siblings he had abandoned, and even the gang he planned to meet later that night. Each revelation struck Kalicharan like a thunderbolt, breaking through his tough exterior. Baba was a college student at the time. Though only 18 years old, Baba had already mastered profound spiritual practices and often visited cremation grounds during the full moon to meditate. Baba looked Kalicharan in the eyes and said, "I know you want my money, but I have something far more valuable to offer you. Would you like to know what it is?"

Kalicharan nodded, curious and confused.

Baba leaned forward. "First, you must clean yourself. Jump into the river and wash yourself, both inside and out. Only then can we talk."

Although skeptical, Kalicharan found himself obeying. Something about Baba's calm yet commanding demeanor disarmed him. He wondered, *Who is this magician, and what does he want from me?*

After washing in the cool waters of the Hooghly, Kalicharan returned, shivering slightly but feeling oddly refreshed. Baba didn't mince words. "You've caused a lot of pain," he began. Then, with unerring precision, he listed Kalicharan's worst deeds: the thefts, the violence, the betrayals. As Baba spoke, Kalicharan's defenses crumbled. Tears streamed down his face, silent yet hopeful of redemption. "If you want to change," Baba continued, "you must follow Yama and Niyama. These principles are your path to redemption. Promise me you will follow them to the best of your ability."

Kalicharan hesitated, but he knew his life was spiraling into chaos. He recognized this as a rare chance for change. Finally, he said, "I promise."

Baba nodded approvingly. "Good. Tonight, I will teach you meditation. It will help you purify your mind and move away from your destructive tendencies." When their session ended, Kalicharan insisted on walking Baba home. He feared nearby thugs might harm this extraordinary young teacher. Upon reaching Baba's residence, Baba turned to Kalicharan and said, "Come back tomorrow." Then, to Kalicharan's astonishment, Baba took out a few rupees from his wallet and handed them to him. "Take this," he said firmly.

Kalicharan was deeply moved. Acts of kindness were foreign to him. The last time he had experienced such warmth was from his mother, whom he had not spoken to in years. For the first time in what felt like an eternity, Kalicharan saw a glimmer of hope that he could change. This was the beginning of Kalicharan's transformation. Baba's compassion, wisdom, and faith in his potential planted the seeds of a new path, one where Kalicharan would leave behind his life of crime and become a seeker of truth.

Qualities of a Good Teacher

The story above is one of my favorite stories in the lore of my guru's past and legacy. It highlights how the right teacher can change your life's course. Baba isn't the only master who transformed a troubled disciple. Many great teachers are credited with having anti-heroes among their students. The Buddha taught Angulimala, the robber and murderer, who carried sliced finger trophies of all his victims around his neck.[1] Kalicharan and Angulimala are more than stories of redemption. They illustrate the power of a teacher who can transform your life and help you reach dreams and goals you never imagined possible.

Though, I never learned directly from Baba, as he had passed away ten years before I discovered his teachings, I still became a devoted student and disciple of Baba's philosophy, thanks to the remarkable teachers he trained during his lifetime. Baba established a vast lineage of monks and nuns, called *acharyas,* who dedicated themselves to spreading his teachings across the globe. These acharyas—teachers who lead by example—are some of the most inspiring mentors I have ever encountered.

One acharya whose friendship influenced my life was Dada Veda, also an author and song writer. In the early 2000s, I traveled to Albania to volunteer at a kindergarten Dada Veda had established. During my time there, I was just a few years into my meditation practice. One of my challenges during this period was learning long Sanskrit chants. Singing these chants from memory would mark a milestone in my journey. However, their complexity made it hard for me to memorize them.

Dada Veda offered unwavering support. Each evening for a month, after our meditation sessions, he would sit with me patiently, helping me master the intricacies of the chants. His approach was meticulous yet compassionate, breaking down the complex verses into manageable segments. He practiced chanting them with me until I could sing them all on my own. Night after night, Dada Veda invested his time and energy in this practice, never showing impatience or frustration. Thanks to him, I finally mastered the chants and can recite them with ease to this day.

I learned a lot from Dada Veda, not only thanks to his patience but also through his book *Wisdom of Tantra* (2016), a book on Baba's teachings. In his book, Dada writes about three kinds of teachers:

The Minimal Teacher. This kind of teacher shares a little knowledge but doesn't stick around to help. They leave the student on their own, which often makes it hard for the student to really use or grow from the lesson.

The Halfway Teacher. This kind does more. They give knowledge and offer some guidance for a while, which is better than the first. But their support usually ends too soon for the student to reach their full potential.

The Committed Teacher. This is the highest kind because they not only give knowledge but also stays with the student until he or she reaches true mastery. This teacher keeps guiding, encouraging, and supporting every step of the way with steady dedication.[2]

The Power (and Danger) of a Teacher

A great teacher nurtures growth, encourages curiosity, and leads by example. They uplift students, guiding them toward their highest potential with patience, wisdom, and integrity. A bad teacher, however, misuses their influence, manipulating, exploiting, or demanding blind obedience. Recognizing the difference between the two is essential for any student seeking true transformation.

A Good Teacher:
- encourages independent thinking
- leads with humility and wisdom
- guides through patience and understanding
- inspires students to grow beyond them
- values the student's success

A Bad Teacher:
- demands unquestioning loyalty
- prioritizes their own ego and power
- uses fear, guilt, or intimidation
- holds students back to maintain control
- seeks personal gain from their followers

The story of Ekalavya from the *Mahabharata*, the ancient Indian epic poem, perfectly illustrates both the power of self-discipline and the danger of choosing the wrong teacher.[3] Ekalavya, a boy from a lower caste, dreamed of becoming a great archer. He sought training from Dronacharya, a renowned teacher, but was cruelly rejected due to his status. However, Ekalavya remained determined. Though he was turned away, he retreated to the forest and sculpted a clay statue of Dronacharya and trained before it, mastering archery through sheer dedication.

One day, Dronacharya saw Ekalavya's incredible skill. A dog had been shot through her nose by Ekalavya's arrow and remained in place, a miraculous sight. Ekalavya attributed his skills to Dronacharya's teachings from the clay statue he had made. But rather than show friendship, Dronacharya demanded *Guru Daksina*, a teacher's fee. Instead of money, he coldly asked for Ekalavya's thumbs, ensuring he would never shoot an arrow again. Without hesitation, Ekalavya severed them, believing it was an act of devotion toward his teacher. But Dronacharya had only sought to eliminate a rival, leaving Ekalavya's talent destroyed.

Ekalavya's story is both inspiring and tragic. His self-discipline was extraordinary, but his blind devotion to an unworthy teacher led to an unjust sacrifice. The lesson is clear: a true teacher uplifts, while a bad teacher exploits.

Success is not simply attributed to finding a teacher. It is also about knowing who is truly worthy of your trust. The search for a good teacher requires you to use careful discernment. While the right mentor can illuminate your path and refine your Vision Seed, a cruel teacher can derail even the most dedicated student.

How to Be a Front-Row Student

Just as important as finding the right guide is ensuring we are ready to learn. In every conventional classroom, there are students who naturally gravitate toward the front row and others who prefer the back. While there are always exceptions, those in the back row are sometimes there because it allows them to be less engaged. They can daydream, scroll on their phones, or avoid eye contact with the teacher. On the other hand, front-row students tend to be there because they value the moment, the opportunity to learn, or the teacher's effort.

Front-row students often demonstrate a deeper level of respect, not just for the teacher as a person but for the teaching itself. This respect fuels their curiosity and focus, making them the most engaged and often the most successful learners. They take advantage of proximity to the teacher, paying close attention to every word, gesture, and nuance. Whether they fully realize it or not, their appreciation for the teaching shapes their growth and understanding.

If you find a teacher who can help you grow your Vision Seed and are eager to see it accomplished, consider being a front-row student for your teacher. Endeavor to stay awake, alert, and fully present, striving to absorb every lesson your teacher imparts. Don't just listen passively. Actively take notes, reflect on the teachings, and work to apply them in your life.

When you find the right mentor, it's natural to want to emulate him or her. Beyond the words he or she speaks, observe how they behave, paying attention to their actions, attitudes, and unspoken wisdom. Internalize these subtle lessons much like a baby learns from watching their parents, absorbing everything from deliberate instructions to unconscious examples. In *Wisdom of Tantra* (2016), Dada Veda shares two vivid metaphors to illustrate two types of students:

The Upside-Down Glass Student. This student is like a glass placed upside down in water. Though surrounded by water, the glass retains nothing when lifted. Similarly, the upside-down glass student engages with knowledge and mentorship but fails to apply what they've learned once the teacher or mentor is no longer there. They are inspired to work, but only on the theory and only in the presence of their teacher.

The Upright Glass Student. This student is like a glass placed upright in water. It fills completely and retains the water even after being removed. The upright glass student not only absorbs guidance from mentors and teachers but also consistently applies it, even when working alone.

Consider a student with a vision of starting a sustainable fashion business. They attend workshops and mentorship sessions, soaking up lessons about marketing, supply chains, and brand building. After each session, they actively put what they've learned into practice, developing prototypes, researching ethical suppliers, and creating a clear business strategy.

Even when their mentor is unavailable, they maintain their momentum, adapting and refining their plans based on ongoing feedback and their own insights. This student exemplifies the qualities of self-motivation and commitment. By taking consistent action and internalizing the lessons, they ensure steady progress toward building their business, whether the mentor is there or not. This student is capable of the most profound learning because he or she comes to embody the lessons he or she receives.

Good students don't just focus on theory and goals; they align their learning and habits with their identity. This idea, inspired by James Clear's *Atomic Habits* (2018), highlights that the key to long-term success isn't just achieving milestones but becoming the kind of person who naturally embodies the habits and teachings needed for success. Instead of saying, *I want to start a successful business*, consider saying, *I am an entrepreneur*. Instead of focusing on completing a task like, *I need to write a business plan*, change your identity to say: *I am someone who writes business plans and makes progress on my business every day.*

By connecting habits to identity, students create sustainable motivation. They no longer rely on external rewards to drive action. Instead, their actions naturally align with who they see themselves becoming.

Learning From a Variety of Educational Tools

In the absence of a personal guide, books, podcasts, online courses, and other resources can serve as valuable resources. Every piece of knowledge, whether from a teacher or an external source, becomes a stepping-stone toward your growth.

When I aim to master a new digital platform, such as optimizing my Youtube presence, my first instinct is to seek out expert advice. I turn to search engines like Google to identify influential figures in the field. I actively search for individuals who have achieved remarkable success, perhaps boasting a substantial following of forty thousand subscribers. I then diligently study their content, immersing myself in their teachings through online courses, blog posts, and YouTube videos. This process of learning from accomplished teachers invariably enhances my own social media strategies.

This principle of seeking expert guidance applies universally. Whether your Vision Seed is to master a complex programming language, excel in a competitive sport, or start your own successful business, the presence of a skilled guide is invaluable. However, before embarking on any journey, it is crucial to have a clear understanding of your destination.

Defining your goals helps you identify the type of guidance you require and where to look for it. If your primary goal is to achieve social media success, you will naturally gravitate towards and connect with mentors who possess expertise in this domain. These teachers are likely found in social media apps. If your aspirations transcend material pursuits and you seek transformation in areas like overcoming anger or cultivating inner peace, your journey will lead you to teachers who specialize in these realms too. This might involve connecting with a therapist, a life coach, or a spiritual mentor who can provide the necessary tools and guidance for your personal growth. These teachers may be found in health clinics, temples, or ancient sites.

The truth is that many of us are more lost than we initially realize. We may believe we know our destination, only to discover that our initial assumptions were misguided. In these instances, teachers we encounter serve a more profound purpose: they help us discover our true destination. Sometimes, the teacher you seek leads you down an unexpected path, one that challenges your assumptions and helps you grow in ways you never anticipated. These teachers are not just instructors. They are catalysts for deeper exploration. They may present opportunities you didn't foresee. True teachers may not always take you where you thought you wanted to go, but they will always lead you to where you need to be.

Steadiness of Mind: Balance, Breath, and Belonging

AT 29, ALEXIS FOUND HERSELF BEHIND BARS after years of dealing drugs. The despair hit hard. She felt shame, regret and thought her life was over. In the early days of her sentence, she felt like she was stuck—no longer heading toward the future. But one question shifted everything: *How can I grow from this experience?*

Instead of letting prison define her, Alexis used it as a turning point. She began reading, journaling, and reflecting on the choices that led her there. Over time, she discovered a passion for writing, using it to process her emotions, tell her story, and find purpose. In that moment of clarity, Alexis showed what it means to cultivate steadiness of mind. Like a pilot regaining control of an aircraft in turbulence, she steadied herself, choosing a safe landing instead of a crash.

Your mind is an extraordinary instrument, wired with the capacity for creativity and analysis. Whether you're crafting a compelling argument, unraveling a complex problem, composing a poem, or dreaming at night, your mind's potential is vast. Yet, this remarkable capacity can often feel just out of reach. Why? Because when left unchecked, the mind can just as easily become a source of confusion and frustration. Furthermore, the mind can get easily overwhelmed at both the highs and lows of everyday life.

Therefore, it becomes important to develop steadiness of mind: the ability to remain centered despite life's uncertainties. Building a steady mind requires practice, just like any other skill. For instance, athletes train their bodies to perform under pressure, and musicians practice for hours to perfect their craft. Similarly, we can cultivate steadiness through intentional exercises that strengthen our mental and emotional resilience.

Balancing Physical, Mental, and Spiritual Needs

Human beings often struggle to maintain balance physically, mentally, and spiritually. This imbalance doesn't happen overnight. It's the result of stressful and traumatic experiences, daily choices, distractions, and competing priorities. Our modern world, with its relentless pace and demands, makes it easy to neglect balancing our needs.

A lot of this imbalance comes from how we're wired as human beings. Our ancestors needed the fight-or-flight response to survive real dangers like wild animals or sudden threats. Our bodies still have that reaction today. The problem is that modern life sets it off in situations that aren't truly life-threatening: a stressful email, an upcoming deadline, or an argument at home. Our hearts race, adrenaline floods our system, and our thoughts spin out of control, even though the danger isn't physical. This old survival mechanism leaves us stuck in high-stress, draining our energy and throwing off our balance.

In yoga philosophy each of the seven chakras, or energy centers, along the spine of the body represent a different cluster of emotions.[1] Balance is often represented through the Root Chakra (*Muladhara*), located at the base of the spine, which is said to govern fundamental desires.

Sometimes Muladhara is called the "chakra of desire" because it governs our most basic needs and drives. But I like to think of it as a framework for balance, as it encompasses a basic spectrum of what makes us whole and guides us toward equilibrium and wellness.

Figure 2
Muladhara Chakra

ARTHA   KAMA

DHARMA   MOKSHA

Figure 2 shows an image of the four-petaled Muladhara Chakra and the four propensities it controls:

- **intellectual desire (Artha):** The pursuit of knowledge, creativity, and problem-solving.
- **physical desire (Kama):** The need for comfort, nourishment, and physical security.
- **spiritual desire (Moksha):** The longing for enlightenment, spiritual connection, and inner peace.
- ***Dharma:*** See the previous chapter: What Being Human Reveals About Your Purpose for an explanation.

Rather than always striving for equal attention to all four propensities in the Muladhara Chakra, balance means recognizing when one area has been neglected and making conscious efforts to realign. Imagine planning your day with this in mind. You may start the day with physical movement, then later engage in an intellectually stimulating activity like reading, and in the evening set aside a few moments for meditation or prayer. Engaging in these activities enables balance of the physical, mental, spiritual realms, helping to steady the mind.

When we cultivate this balance, we avoid the extremes of overindulgence or neglect.

On the other hand, consider a typical day in the life of someone preoccupied mostly with physical needs. They wake up and immediately think about their breakfast, rushing to prepare food before hurrying off to work. Throughout the day, they focus on tasks to earn money, their thoughts revolving around paying bills, affording better clothing, or planning their next meal. After work, they might unwind with entertainment or social activities that prioritize comfort and pleasure, such as drinking alcohol or binge-watching TV. Meanwhile, little to no time is set aside for intellectual development, such as reading or learning, and even less for spiritual pursuits. Over time, this lopsided focus leads to a sense of dissatisfaction. The senses may be stimulated, but the intellect and spirit remains malnourished, leaving a void that physical comforts alone cannot fill.

It is important to note that it is not solely our individual fault when we become overly preoccupied with physical needs. Basic needs are not guaranteed in a capitalist society. Long work hours, rising costs, and societal pressure to accumulate material wealth leave little room for intellectual growth or spiritual exploration. Modern capitalist systems often forces people to prioritize survival over fulfillment, perpetuating cycles of imbalance and leaving many unable to maintain holistic wellness.

Balancing Emotions

You experience a rich spectrum of emotions: joy, anger, jealousy, sadness, hope, surrender, love, and so many others. These emotions color your life. They create your thoughts and the way you respond to your surroundings, yet they can also throw you off balance if mismanaged. A steady mind isn't one that suppresses emotions but one that acknowledges them, understands their role, and navigates them with gentle awareness.

The Pixar film *Inside Out* (2015), directed and co-written by Pete Docter, offers a wonderful illustration of this idea. *Inside Out* follows an 11-year-old girl, Riley, as she struggles with a hard move to a new city. Inside her mind, five emotions—joy, sadness, anger, fear, and disgust—compete for control. At first, joy dominates, attempting to keep Riley happy at all costs. However, as the story unfolds, each emotion reveals a purpose. Sadness, for instance, plays a crucial role in helping Riley process change, express vulnerability, and seek support.[2] The film teaches an essential lesson: emotional steadiness doesn't mean eliminating difficult feelings; it means recognizing each emotion's value and maintaining balance.

To cultivate a steady mind, we must see emotions not as obstacles but as signals. When in balance, emotions guide us toward better decisions, deeper relationships, and personal growth. However, when one emotion dominates unchecked, it can disrupt our well-being. Let's explore three key emotions and how they can be valued rather than suppressed:

Sadness. Although sadness is often misunderstood as something to be avoided, it serves a vital function. It deepens empathy, fosters reflection, and signals when we need support. However, when sadness lingers unchecked, it can lead to isolation or hopelessness. When we feel sad, we can ask, *What do I need to accept or change that is making me feel this way?*

Anger. When anger is balanced, it can be a powerful motivator for justice and transformation. It signals when boundaries have been crossed or when something in our environment needs to change. However, unchecked anger can cloud judgment and lead to destructive actions. A steady mind doesn't suppress anger but channels it constructively, asking: *How can I express this emotion in a way that leads to growth rather than harm?*

Fear. Often regarded as a survival instinct, fear sharpens our awareness and protects us from harm. But when it overpowers us, it fuels anxiety, avoidance, and self-doubt. A person who fears rejection, for example, might avoid pursuing meaningful relationships or career opportunities, mistaking imagined failure for inevitable reality. Instead of letting fear dictate action, we can reframe it: *What am I imagining that is causing me fear?*

Next time you experience a potent emotion, pause and ask:

- *What is this emotion trying to tell me?*
- *Is my response balanced, or am I letting this feeling take control?*
- *How can I use this emotion as a tool rather than an obstacle?*

By viewing emotions as allies rather than enemies, we cultivate a steadiness that allows us to move through life's ups and downs with clarity and resilience.

The Rhythm of Breath: A Mirror to the Mind

Dada Vishvarupananda, or Dada V as his students call him, is a senior monk in my guru's lineage and my meditation teacher. For over twenty-five years, he has been an incredible friend and guide. Through both his direct teachings and the way he lives with humility, joy, and compassion, I have learned countless lessons that continue to shape my life.

For example, I recall attending a talk he gave at his home in Rockville, Maryland, where he taught our community secrets of the breath, or *Pranayama*. Pranayama is the yogic practice of breath control. In his lesson, Dada V showed us how Pranayama could serve not only as a tool for meditation but also as a powerful method for emotional regulation in daily life.

Breath is a mirror to the mind. When we are calm, our breath has the potential to be steady and deep. When we are anxious or agitated, our breath becomes rapid and shallow. This is not just a yogic idea. It's a scientific fact. Modern research confirms that the way we breathe directly influences our nervous system, shifting us between states of stress (the sympathetic nervous system) and relaxation (the parasympathetic nervous system).[3]

Dada V explained how simple changes like breathing through your nose, slowing your exhalation, or lengthening the pause between your breaths could regulate emotions and restore balance to the mind. He taught that just as the mind shapes the breath, the breath can shape the mind.

There are two key divisions of the autonomic nervous system. The sympathetic nervous system is the body's response to stress. It prepares you to react to danger by speeding up the heart rate, quickening the breath, and flooding the body with adrenaline. The parasympathetic nervous system is the body's response to safety and recovery. It restores calm by slowing the heart rate, relaxing the muscles, and bringing the body back into balance.[4]

In modern life, many people get stuck in a stressful (sympathetic) state, constantly on edge, reacting to emails, deadlines, and worries as if they were life-threatening. The problem is we rarely activate the parasympathetic system intentionally through breathing. Breathwork is a tool to do exactly that: to shift the body into a state of balance.

Pranayama Techniques for Getting Calm and Focused

Below are three simple Pranayama (breath control) exercises you can practice anytime to steady your mind:

Lengthening the Exhalation (Calming the Nervous System). When you breathe out longer than you breathe in, you activate the Vagus Nerve, which signals the body to relax.[5] The vagus nerve is the longest and most complex of the ten cranial nerves that connects the brain with the rest of the body.[6] This is a powerful technique for easing stress taught by Dada V. Use this when you're feeling anxious or overwhelmed. It's a natural reset button that can also help you sleep better:

1. Inhale deeply through your nose for three counts.
2. Exhale slowly through your mouth for four to six counts.
3. Repeat for a few minutes, focusing on extending your exhalation.

Finding Stability in the Breath (Building Emotional Resilience). This practice trains the breath to be smooth and even, which in turn steadies the mind. Use this during high-stress situations, like before an important conversation or when navigating conflict:

1. Breathe in through your nose for four counts.
2. Breathe out through your mouth for four counts.
3. Keep the breath steady and consistent, like an unbroken wave.

Kumbhaka: **The Space Between the Breath (Cultivating Inner Stillness).** In yoga, the pause between breaths is called Kumbhaka. It represents a state of deep stillness and presence. Instead of focusing only on inhaling and exhaling, this technique invites you to rest in the silent space between breaths. The pauses create a sense of equanimity. Use this to remain steady even in moments of uncertainty:

1. Inhale through your nose for four counts.
2. Hold the breath gently for four counts.
3. Exhale through your mouth for four counts.
4. Pause for a moment before inhaling again.

By cultivating awareness of the breath, you cultivate awareness of the mind. With practice, steadiness of breath becomes steadiness of being.

Inferiority Complexes

CeCe Olisa, a motivational speaker and co-founder of The Curvy-Con, grew up passionate about performing dance, theater, and singing. Encouraged by her parents, she believed in her talent. But as she got older, societal pressures about body image chipped away at her confidence. A teacher once told her mother that CeCe couldn't join the elite dance group because she didn't have a "dancer's body." Later in high school, a drama teacher denied her a leading role, claiming it was unrealistic for someone her size.[7]

These experiences left CeCe discouraged. She quit auditioning, took a corporate job, and struggled with an eating disorder. But eventually, she realized that waiting to be a certain size before living fully wasn't the answer. She started sharing her journey online, celebrating body positivity and self-acceptance. Today, CeCe's message is simple: your worth is not conditional. You don't need to change who you are to deserve success, happiness, or love.

CeCe's weight loss journey is an inspiring case study showing how inferiority complexes become ingrained in the mind. Inferiority complexes stem from persistent feelings of self-doubt and unworthiness, often rooted in shame. These feelings create an imbalanced mind, making it difficult to maintain confidence and clarity. To cultivate steadiness, we must recognize where these beliefs originate and challenge them with self-awareness and action.[8]

Areas of Shame

Researcher Brené Brown, author of *Daring Greatly: How the Courage to Be Vulnerable Transforms the Way we Live, Love, Parent, and Lead* (2012), describes shame as "the intensely painful feeling of believing that we are flawed and therefore unworthy of love and belonging." Shame creates inferiority complexes by convincing us that our shortcomings define us. People experience shame in different areas of life, but according to Brené Brown, they often fall into a few broad themes:

Appearance and Body Image. Feeling inadequate due to weight, height, age, or beauty standards can cause a person to judge their worth based on how their body looks rather than who they are as a whole person.

Career and Success. Financial struggles, job loss, or not meeting societal definitions of success can lead someone to feel like they have failed or fallen behind, even when these outcomes are influenced by circumstances beyond their control.

Relationships and Social Belonging. Feeling unworthy of love due to past rejections, divorce, family conflicts, or a lack of close connections can create a deep sense of isolation and disconnection from others.

Past Mistakes and Regrets. Shame from failures, legal troubles, addiction, or choices that did not align with one's values can cause a person to remain stuck in self-blame rather than allowing space for growth and change.

Regardless of where it manifests, shame convinces us that we are less than and that others have it figured out while we remain inadequate. The truth is, everyone wrestles with insecurities. The key is learning to see them not as barriers but as opportunities for growth. To break free from an inferiority complex, consider these steps as taught in CeCe Olisa's 2018 TEDx Talk:

Step One: Identify Your Perceived Obstacle. What do you believe is holding you back? CeCe thought it was her weight. For you, it might be a lack of experience, past failures, or financial struggles. Naming the obstacle removes its power.

Step Two: Reframe the Narrative. Instead of thinking, "I can't do this because of _____," ask, "How can I succeed despite _____?" CeCe stopped seeing her size as a limitation and focused on embracing her strengths.[8]

Step Three: Take Action Now. What can you do now to move toward your goals? Don't wait until you "feel ready" to pursue your goals. Confidence comes from doing, not waiting.

Step Four: Speak Shame Out Loud. Who can you share your story with? Sharing your struggles with trusted friends, therapists, or mentors can help dismantle shame's grip.

By shifting to a growth mindset and taking small, courageous steps, we see that worthiness is not something to be earned. It is something we already possess.

Superiority Complexes

A superiority complex arises when someone believes they are inherently better than others, because of intelligence, status, religion, or personal achievements. While this mindset may provide a temporary sense of confidence, it often leads to disconnection, judgment, and isolation. At its core, superiority is often just another mask for insecurity, built to shield us from feelings of self-doubt or inadequacy.

Human beings are wired for belonging. Throughout history, group identity has played a crucial role in survival, providing protection, shared resources, and social connection. However, this instinct can also create division. The moment we feel sentiment for our group over another, we tend to assume our group is better than others.

The minimal group paradigm studies of the 1970s show that even in artificial settings, people quickly develop in-group bias.[9] In one experiment, strangers were randomly assigned to groups, and within minutes, they began favoring their own group over others, even though there were no real differences between them. Imagine how this bias intensifies when tied to deeply held identities like nationality, religion, culture, gender, personal philosophy, race, or class. We often build walls rather than bridges, consciously or unconsciously.

Even within spiritual communities, I've seen superiority complexes emerge. Some practitioners believe their meditation style is the only true path, looking down on others with different approaches. Similarly, in religious settings, I've encountered groups convinced that only their faith holds the key to salvation, dismissing others as misguided or unworthy. But true wisdom does not seek to prove itself superior. Rather, true wisdom strives to uplift others.

The Importance of Humility and Service

I once had a student who approached me to talk about her career path. She didn't phrase her question in the typical—"What should I do with my life?"—kind of way. Instead, she asked a deeper question, *"I want to learn what God wants me to do with my life?"* Her words reflected humility and a willingness to step beyond personal gain to align with something greater.

Regardless of whether one has a spiritual approach or not, at the heart of one's Vision Seed or career choice is asking: *How can I use my skills to serve, rather than simply to succeed?* Sometimes our pursuits are motivated by attempting to prove our greatness rather than contributing to the whole. Here are steps to avoid superiority complexes:

Step One: Shift from Comparison to Contribution. Instead of measuring yourself against others, focus on how your abilities can be of service.

Step Two: Practice Gratitude. Regularly reflect on the people, experiences, and circumstances that have helped you grow instead of believing you accomplished everything all by yourself. This will help you minimize the vanity of your ego.

Step Three: Seek Diverse Perspectives. Surround yourself with people from different backgrounds and listen with an open mind.

Step Four: Stay Curious, Not Certain. When we assume we know everything, our growth and our ability to listen end. Approach all of your obstacles with the mindset of a lifelong learner.[10]

Superiority creates barriers; humility builds connection. By choosing to focus on service rather than status, we move from seeking validation to creating meaningful impact. True strength is found not in proving we are better, but in recognizing that we are all works-in-progress, learning together.

The world will continue to shift around you through uncertainty, setbacks, and difficult moments. However, with a steady mind, you remain anchored like a deep-rooted tree that bends with the wind but never breaks. Fear, doubt, or external pressures do not easily sway you when your mind is steady. Instead, you recognize emotions without being consumed by them, adapt to change without losing your center, and approach obstacles as opportunities for growth rather than setbacks.

Embracing Self-Restraint:
Moving Beyond Impulse

DURING ONE OF HIS TALKS on the topic of embracing self-restraint, Dada V shared the following wisdom:

> The senses are like wild horses. Left unchecked, they pull you in every direction—toward cravings, toward distractions, toward whatever feels good in the moment. But if you learn to guide them, to master them, they become powerful tools, serving your highest purpose instead of leading you astray.[1]

Self-restraint is one of the most misunderstood qualities of success. To some, it sounds restrictive, like a set of rigid rules designed to suppress joy. But in reality, self-restraint is about freedom. It's the ability to make conscious choices rather than being controlled by impulses, distractions, or momentary pleasures. It's what allows us to stay focused on long-term goals rather than chasing every fleeting desire.

Don't Eat the Marshmallow!

Psychologists have long recognized that the ability to manage impulses can shape the course of a person's life.

The marshmallow test from the 1960s involved putting a four-year-old in a room with a marshmallow placed right in front of them.[2] A Stanford researcher would tell the child something like, "You can eat this marshmallow now, or if you wait until I come back, I'll give you a second one. Two marshmallows instead of one!" Then the researcher would leave, and the kid would be alone with the marshmallow and their thoughts.

Some kids in the experiment distracted themselves by singing songs, closing their eyes, or turning away to avoid temptation. Others gave in almost immediately, popping the marshmallow into their mouths. The researchers were secretly observing everything, curious to see what would happen.

Years later, the researchers followed up with these children as teenagers. The kids who had resisted eating the marshmallow performed better academically, had higher self-esteem, and were less likely to engage in risky behaviors.[3] Those who couldn't wait struggled more in school, had lower confidence, and were more prone to issues like substance use.

This study shows that kids who show self-restraint at a young age are more likely to achieve success later in life. Of course, resisting temptation may not have been the only factor attributed to these kids' success. Other helpful factors, such as wealth or a stable family life, may have also supported them. The test still reveals that resisting temptation is not about sheer willpower alone. It is about finding ways to manage impulses, to pause between desire and acting. The children who succeeded were the ones who used strategies like distractions, imagination, or self-talk to help themselves through the waiting.

That same principle applies to us as adults. We may not be staring down a marshmallow, but we face countless temptations every day: junk food, social media, alcohol, or the pull of old habits. Like those children, we can strengthen our self-restraint not by demanding perfection, but by using simple, effective strategies that give us room to choose differently and delay instant gratification.

It is not worth asking ourselves how we can be free from temptations because we know we will always face temptations. The important questions are: *Who is in control? Do I act based on my deepest values, or do I allow passing impulses to dictate my path?* Often the problem is not a lack of willpower but something deeper. When you reach for "the marshmallow," it might not be because you lack self-control. It may be because you're trying to fill an emotional void, escape discomfort, or soothe an insecurity.

The Deeper Issues Behind a Lack of Discipline

One of my students once wrote about how a simple way to relax turned into a huge crutch. At first, he would come home from school, sit down to play a video game, and tell himself he would only play one round. But one game became two, then three, and soon whole afternoons disappeared without him even noticing. His continuous gaming stretched into months, then nearly a year of his life was consumed in that cycle. He described how the pull of the game felt stronger than his own willpower, how stopping seemed impossible even when he wanted to. Eventually, his parents had to step in with a serious intervention. That moment, although difficult, finally broke the spell and gave him the chance to reclaim his time and his focus.

My student's experience wasn't just a problem with self-discipline. It pointed to a deeper need. Maybe he felt disconnected. Perhaps his social circle wasn't giving him the support he needed, or he was grappling with feelings of inadequacy. These emotional gaps can make self-restraint much harder. In these cases, the solution isn't just gritting your teeth and pushing through. Instead, you should address the root cause.

My Early Experience with Drugs

When I was 12 years old, many of my friends had already started experimenting with drugs. Their stories stirred my curiosity, and I started experimenting with them too. Beneath that curiosity lived something I could not yet name. Perhaps I wanted to belong. I wanted to share what my friends were doing. Looking back, I believe I wanted to ease the emptiness I often felt at home.

My mother must have noticed my new interest in drugs and what my friends were doing. That's why, during Christmas Break, she took me to Bolivia. At first, I thought it was just a holiday visit, but then she sat me down and said, "Why don't you just stay here?" I was shocked. My friends, my life, everything I knew was back in the United States, but she convinced me to stay for a year. In hindsight, that decision may have saved me.

In Bolivia, I found something I didn't even realize I was missing: a strong, loving community and family ties. My aunt and uncle became like second parents and my cousins like siblings. I lived with them once already for close to a year, the first time my mother sent me when I was 8 months old. My grandparents lived nearby, and my grandmother's unconditional love created a deep sense of security. The neighborhood kids welcomed me, and my friendship with Sergio, my best friend, who played guitar, inspired me tremendously.

By the time I returned home, my interest in drugs had simply disappeared. Not because I had been scared straight, but because something had shifted inside me. Something had filled the void. This experience taught me something crucial: addiction or escape in drugs isn't just about the substance. It's about the underlying need that drives someone toward it.

The Deeper Causes of Addiction

In the book *Chasing the Scream: The First and Last Days of the War on Drugs* (2016), the author Johann Hari argues that addiction is not primarily caused by the chemical hooks of a drug. Rather, it is caused by a lack of emotional connection and a lack of purpose. He points out that societies often treat addiction as a failure of self-control, punishing addicts instead of addressing the root causes: isolation, trauma, and unmet emotional needs.

The War on Drugs, which began in the early 1970s, only made this worse. Instead of offering support and healing, it criminalized addiction, turning a public health crisis into a battle against the very people who needed help the most. This approach pushed drug users further into the shadows, stripping them of dignity and access to treatment.

Singer and jazz icon Billie Holiday's tragic story is a perfect example. Holiday had suffered from addiction since the age of fourteen, when she worked as a sex worker alongside her mother and was raped day after day.[4] Later in life, she became a target of the FBI, not only because of her heroin use but also because of her protest song *Strange Fruit,* which shed light on the lynchings suffered by African Americans.[5] When she was hospitalized in 1959, her body failing, authorities even stationed guards at her door, ensuring she could not access the medical care she needed. She died not just from addiction, but from a system that saw punishment as the solution to suffering.

When we approach addiction with compassion rather than shame and see it not as a moral failing but as a symptom of deeper wounds, we open the door to real healing. This applies not just to drug addiction, but to any form of destructive habit. Whether it's alcohol, compulsive eating, excessive social media use, or even toxic relationships, the pattern is the same.

At its core, struggles with self-restraint can stem from unmet emotional needs, trauma, or isolation. Reaching out to others, cultivating supportive relationships, and fostering a sense of belonging are critical components of recovery. Whether it's reconnecting with family, seeking help from a trusted mentor, or joining a supportive community, these connections provide the emotional foundation necessary for meaningful change. In the words of Johan Hari (2016), the real takeaway from all of this is: "The opposite of addiction is not sobriety. The opposite of addiction is connection."

Strengthening Your Mental Reins

Close your eyes and visualize the times in ancient history when chariots raced across battlefields. Picture a charioteer gripping the reins tightly as powerful horses surged forward. Imagine navigating your life as if it were one of these chariots. The charioteer represents you, the reins symbolize your mind, and the horses are your senses and impulses. If the horses are unruly and the reins weak, the chariot veers off course, unable to reach its destination. In this analogy, the reins need to be strong, and the horses disciplined to follow the charioteer's guidance.

Now, picture yourself trying to save money for a trip, yet every time you walk past a coffee shop, your senses (smell, taste, and desire) beckon you inside for an overpriced latte. You see the welcoming coffee shop sign. You smell the warm coffee. Your tongue craves the flavor of the cappuccino. Your rational mind knows skipping the coffee aligns with your goal, but the cravings for comfort and indulgence keep pulling you off track, like wild horses. Without the discipline of mental discernment, sensory distractions like these accumulate and derail your larger objectives.

Discernment as the Key to Guiding Your Impulses

Discernment, or *Viveka* in Sanskrit, allows you to pause and weigh your options. It becomes the tool that strengthens the reins and brings the horses under control. It's the voice in your mind asking, *Is this hazelnut cappuccino worth all the sugar going into my body?* With practice, discernment grows, helping you guide your impulses rather than being led by them.

Strengthening your mental reins isn't about suppressing or denying your senses. Instead, seek to guide them with purpose, despite the possibility of having weaknesses. Sometimes, we make the wrong choices or let our impulses take over, but that doesn't mean we should respond with harsh self-punishment. Ascetic *sadhus* found in India willingly endure severe austerities to transcend worldly attachments.

Some take extreme measures, such as physical self-mortification, to control their impulses and avoid sensory distractions. Baba would say that such practices miss the point.

Self-restraint isn't about annihilating the senses or denying their existence. It's about mastering them with purpose and intention. You don't need to destroy the horses to control the chariot. You simply need stronger reins and better training. Similarly, if you find you are making the wrong choices in life, acknowledge your mistakes, learn from them, and make choices that are in alignment with your values.

At the heart of self-control is the ability to discern what truly matters. Imagine a toddler who, without a second thought, walks around the living room with no clothes on while company is present. At that age, there is no sense of social appropriateness or boundaries. However, as the child grows older, he or she develops an understanding that walking around naked is inappropriate. This growth reflects the natural human capacity for discernment, the ability to recognize what is appropriate and what aligns with societal norms or personal values. Discernment, as a natural propensity, becomes a conscious tool that guides us toward well-being and meaningful choices.

Developing discernment starts with understanding the natural tendencies of your senses and organs. Your stomach craves food, your tongue seeks flavor, and your eyes are drawn to visual beauty. These impulses are not inherently bad. They are part of being human. The challenge is ensuring they serve you rather than control you. Discernment allows you to enjoy life's pleasures responsibly, without harming others nor losing sight of your goals.

Three Types of Discernment Taught by Dada V

Discernment and Core Values. One way we can guide our decisions is through a value system. Imagine someone who believes deeply in the principle of environmental sustainability. This person lives by the value of reducing waste. When they're at a store, they consistently bring fiber shopping bags to avoid single-use plastic bags. These habits help this person maintain healthy self-restraint, rooted in the Core Value of sustainability.

Discernment and Universal Truths. In earlier chapters of this part of the book, we discussed pursuing universal truth as a Principle of Success. My meditation teacher Dada V once shared a personal experience that brings light to how embracing universal truths can inspire us to live and act differently. Yogic monks, like Dada, often meditate in cemeteries to reflect on the impermanence of life and other fundamental truths. Cemeteries are stark reminders that everything changes and everything dies. They are also quiet and usually have little distractions.

Once in India, he meditated at a cremation ground after asking for permission from the caretaker, who allowed him to sit there. During the meditation, to his surprise, the smell of burning flesh filled the air. For Dada V, this was bizarre yet profound. He recounted that he directly experienced the smell of impermanence, the undeniable reality that the body will die. He was reminded to focus on what is permanent and not cling to what is temporary.

Similarly, consider how often we take our loved ones for granted, acting as though they will always be there. Sometimes, in moments of frustration, we yell at those we care about, forgetting the fundamental truth that the person we are upset with is far greater and more important than the mistake that provoked our anger. Grounding discernment in universal truths provides a compass for navigating life's challenges. It reminds us to prioritize what truly matters, to approach relationships with kindness, and to act in ways that reflect our deeper understanding of reality.

Another universal truth that can guide our actions is remembering that we always exist in relationship to something else. This awareness helps us not view another person as an object but to see the other, even a stranger, as someone with whom we are in relationship with in the present space. The other person has entered our mind, so in this moment we exist in relationship to this person.

Think of the multiple ways you exist in relationship to something else—you and the flower, you and the tree, you and the bird, or you and the lake. At all times, you can experience life as a journey in relationality. Your sense of sight alone may prompt you to objectify another person. But with a deeper outlook, you can see the Universe in the person you are sharing space with. You can honor the divine synchronicity that has placed you and the other person in the same time and place. By applying this philosophy, your actions become aligned with care and awareness.

Discerning Thoughts. Thoughts are representations of reality, but they are not reality itself. Imagine you're looking at a map of your hometown. The map might show the streets, landmarks, and even your own house, but it isn't the actual town. The map is just a representation. Thoughts are constructed from raw materials: memories, experiences, societal impressions, cultural conditioning, or even religious beliefs. These impressions are embedded in your psyche and serve as the raw material for your thoughts.

It is important to recognize the progression of thoughts. There's always an initial thought that sets a course of action or obsessive thinking, such as an impulse to eat ice cream in the middle of the night or a wave of regret triggered by doubt or fear. The initial thought, then, has subsequent thoughts. If you are in a dark room late at night in your house, an initial thought might be: *Oh my God, something's going to jump out at me or attack me.* Now, the second thought could escalate things: *I read the other day that someone was attacked in their home. If something happens to me here, no one will find me for hours, and I'll just lie here, helpless.*

This chain of thought takes on a life of its own. The key is not to let the initial thought spiral into a second, third, or fourth thought. Instead, cut off the first thought immediately. Dismiss it or let it go, recognizing that it's not relevant or helpful to your life at that moment. Remember, thoughts are not inherently true. Discernment allows us to evaluate them critically, separating truth from illusion. By monitoring our thoughts, we gain greater control over the actions that arise from them.

Caring for the Body: Fuel, Movement, and Reverence

A FEW YEARS AGO, I found myself in the mountains of Pumaqanchi, Peru at 3,600 meters above sea level. I had traveled there for a spiritual retreat and would meet my teacher, Tupac T'ito Kuntur, a *Paqo Altomesayoc*, an Andean elder rooted in the Quechua shamanic tradition. At this high altitude, bearing the coldest nights required the use of seven or more blankets. So while I went seeking spiritual development, I first found a lesson in taking care of the body.

Pumaqanchi is not a place where you casually sip cold water. In fact, we were advised never to drink anything cold. The risk of shocking the body in that climate is real. Some participants arrived prepared with thermoses to keep warm liquids by their side. I didn't. Trusting the advice of the group, I avoided water rather than drinking it cold during our outings. One day, we gathered at the edge of a sacred lake to receive a teaching. Tupac spoke for nearly an hour, sharing his wisdom, after showing us a ritual to cleanse our spiritual tools.

Unfortunately, I couldn't take any of it in. My mind was foggy, and my chest was tight from my acid reflux symptoms, causing stress. I wasn't present. I was annoyed. My body was shouting for care, and I had to stifle its noise out of politeness for the duration of the talk. Afterward, I approached Tupac quietly and told him what

I had been feeling. I explained the acid reflux I was struggling with and had struggled with back home for a long time, and how the cold and dehydration were making it worse. I apologized for my distracted demeanor and told him I needed to go into town to buy a thermos.

"Great! Very good, brother," he said warmly. "Yes, you need to take care of your *manqo swasi* (body in the Quechua language). Go buy a thermos to give your body what it needs. If you don't take care of your body, you will block yourself." He reminded me that any progress I make in life can be derailed by a body that needs care.

His words landed with weight. I had come to receive spiritual teachings, and here they were, in the form of a reminder I'd heard all my life from my mother and grandmother through nagging voices: "Take care of your body. Take an extra sweater just in case." Suddenly, it all clicked. We often chase emotional breakthroughs or spiritual growth, forgetting that our body is our first place of safety. If it breaks down, our ambitions collapse with it. Just as a clean signal needs a working radio to be heard, our purpose needs a healthy body to be expressed.

Listening to your body's needs should be done with the same reverence that you listen for your higher calling. Dehydration, lack of sleep, poor nutrition, and burnout are not just health concerns. They are purpose disruptors. When we ignore the body's signals, we create blockages. Our energy wanes. Our focus scatters. Slowly, we lose access to the deep wisdom that only a balanced system can receive.

When we're young, it's easy to believe we are invincible. We eat what we want, push our limits, and ignore signs of fatigue or stress. However, as we age, we understand we can no longer take stamina and health for granted.

Fuel for Alignment

Your body is a biological machine. Like a car or an airplane, it requires fuel to function. I am often amazed at how cautious people are to put the exact grade of engine oil or gasoline into their automobiles but completely lack any caution for fueling their own bodies. We're driven more by the instant gratification of food than by a thoughtful, scientific selection of what foods will give us the most energy, enhance our lives, and truly make us thrive. Think of your body as a high-performance vehicle. If you want to win the race, you need to fuel it with the best possible energy. Similarly, if you want to achieve your goals and be the best version of yourself, you need to provide your body with the nutrients it needs.

Food is the body's fuel. People are often very sensitive around the topic of what they should eat. With countless recommendations and diets out there, it's overwhelming to decide which one is correct. However, the bottom line is that what you eat matters. You should choose the best food for your body and goals, providing it with the nutrients and energy it needs to function at its best.

Highly processed foods loaded with salt or sugar may give you a quick energy boost but often leave you feeling guilty or sluggish in the long run. In contrast, nutritious whole foods are the healthiest options for the body. These include fresh fruits like apples, berries, and oranges, which are packed with vitamins and antioxidants. Vegetables such as spinach, kale, and broccoli provide essential nutrients like fiber, iron, and calcium. Whole grains, such as quinoa, oats, and brown rice, offer sustained energy and improve digestion. Healthy fats found in foods like avocados, nuts, seeds, and olive oil support brain function and reduce inflammation. By choosing wholesome, unprocessed foods, you can fuel your body effectively, sustain energy, and enhance mental clarity.[1]

Food is a life source, not just something we consume for pleasure or habit. Every time we eat, we merge our life force with another. Whether it's a tomato or a handful of almonds, that energy becomes part of our own. This realization invites a deeper question: Are we choosing foods that are most alive, most energizing, and most aligned with our well-being? If you walk into a supermarket, what you're really seeing is an entire building filled with different life sources. Some are fresh and vibrant. Others are processed, depleted, and artificially withheld from decaying.

What questions go through your mind as you choose food? Maybe you think: *Is this tasty?* How about: *Is this alive?* Fresh, vibrant foods—those closest to the Earth and recently harvested—carry a kind of energetic integrity. These are the foods that support our growth, our clarity, and our connection to nature. However, vitality isn't only about freshness. It's also about relationships. It is important to ask: *How was this food grown or raised? Was it nurtured with care or stripped of dignity? What is the global ecological impact of the food I choose to eat?*

When we consume animals who lived in confinement and were slaughtered brutally, we are not just ingesting nutrients. We are absorbing the energy of suffering. That energy affects us, whether or not we recognize it. Many people turn to organic plant-based eating because they believe plants are closer to the Earth and experience less suffering. A mango harvested at its peak or a lettuce leaf still wet with dew doesn't experience pain the way an animal visibly does. Although, it offers its life nonetheless.

Choosing what we eat becomes more than a nutritional decision. It becomes a question of ethics and resonance, too. Michael Pollan, author of *The Omnivore's Dilemma* (2007), writes:

> 'Eating is an agricultural act,' as Wendell Berry famously said. It is also an ecological act, and a political act, too. Though much has been done to obscure this simple fact, how and what we eat determines to a great extent the use we make of the world—and what is to become of it.

When we approach food conscientiously, asking what is most life-giving, not just to us, but to the Earth and all her beings, we begin to eat not only for survival but also for alignment.

Food and Energy

When you eat, your body shifts its focus to processing the food you've consumed. This process, while necessary, is energy intensive. Your digestive system generates heat and uses significant resources to break down food and absorb nutrients. The heavier or more complex the food, the more energy this process requires, leaving you with less energy for other tasks.

For example, heavily processed foods, sugary snacks, or large portions of red meat can burden your digestive system. While you might experience a quick energy boost, it may be followed by a crash as your body struggles to process these foods. Light, natural foods such as fruits, leafy greens, and whole grains are much easier to digest. They allow your body to conserve energy, leaving you feeling lighter and more energized. This conserved energy can then be devoted to your Vision Seed or to what truly matters—living a long life with family and loved ones.

The key to a healthy diet is balance. Even the most nutritious foods can cause problems if you overeat or ignore the body's signals. Listen to your body and experiment to find what works best for you. Scientists and nutritionists can provide general guidelines, but ultimately, it's about understanding your unique needs. Start by experimenting with different foods and observing how they make you feel. Does a particular meal leave you energized or sluggish? Do you feel satisfied or bloated?

Keep track of these experiences to discover the foods that best support your body and lifestyle. You might find that a breakfast of oatmeal with fresh berries and nuts gives you sustained energy, while a sugary pastry leaves you feeling tired by mid-morning. Not everyone's body reacts to food in the same way; two people might eat the same sugary treat, like ice cream, but one may gain weight more easily than the other.

This difference often comes down to how their bodies handle glucose. Different individuals have varying glucose level reactions to the same foods.[2] Continuous glucose monitoring (CGM) devices track glucose levels in real time, offering insights into how certain meals or snacks may cause spikes in blood sugar.[3] Identifying these sugar spikes, which can contribute to weight gain and energy crashes, helps individuals make more mindful and informed dietary choices based on their bodies' unique needs.

Making changes to your diet can feel overwhelming. Our eating habits are deeply rooted, and changing them often feels like an enormous task. It's important to remember that big changes often seem more complicated than they really are. The key is to take the first step and start building momentum. It's also important to acknowledge that not everyone has the same economic privilege of accessing fresh, healthy foods. In fact, while you read this, you may be in a tough situation where your choices are very limited. In these cases, the focus should be on making the best choices possible within your means and capacity.

Movement

Aside from the importance of food, it is essential to consider physical exercise as another key aspect of caring for the body. Chelsey Luger and Thosh Collins, life partners and co-authors of *The Seven Circles: Indigenous Teachings for Living Well* (2022), bring a unique perspective to this topic, blending wellness with cultural wisdom. Luger is a writer and wellness advocate from the Turtle Mountain Band of Chippewa Indians. Collins is a trainer and wellness consultant from the Onk Akimel O'odham (Pima) and Wah-Zha-Zhi (Osage) Nations. They are on a mission to promote holistic health within their families and in their communities.

In *The Seven Circles: Indigenous Teachings for Living Well (2022)*, they emphasize that wellness is far more than physical appearance. Rather, it's about creating harmony in all aspects of life. Luger and Collins prefer the term "movement" over "fitness." They believe "fitness" often emphasizes aesthetics or performance, whereas "movement" reflects the deeper, universal importance of physical activity. Movement, they suggest, isn't about striving for a perfect body or following trends. Instead, it's about reconnecting with our bodies and using them in ways that honor their natural design.[4]

Luger and Collins's teachings are rooted in Indigenous traditions that view the body as an interconnected system and movement as a natural practice for everyone. Following this, they encourage us to engage the entire body during movement. This approach nurtures every part of ourselves, including the parts we might neglect, and strengthens us for everyday physical tasks. For instance, think about the mobility and coordination needed to kneel while playing with a child or the endurance involved in shoveling snow. Exercise should mirror the functional movements that serve practical purposes.

This approach to movement is called functional strength training, a type of exercise that mimics everyday movements to improve your body's ability to perform everyday tasks.[5] Under this method, movement and exercise can fulfill both an aesthetic dimension and practical life needs. Luger and Collins (2022) highlight seven fundamental movement patterns:

Push:

- **exercise examples:** push-ups, overhead shoulder press, or chest press
- **functional examples:** pushing a shopping cart or someone in a wheelchair

Pull:

- **exercise examples:** dumbbell rows, pull-ups, or seated cable rows
- **functional examples:** pulling a backpack onto your shoulder or dragging a garbage bin

Squat:

- **exercise examples:** bodyweight squats, goblet squats, or barbell back squats
- **functional examples:** sitting in chair or lowering to pick up a child

Lunge:

- **exercise examples:** forward lunges, walking lunges, or Bulgarian split squats
- **functional examples:** kneeling to garden or reaching to tie a shoelace

Hip Hinge:

- **exercise examples:** deadlifts, kettlebell swings, or good mornings
- **functional examples:** bending over to lift a laundry basket or shovel soil

Rotate:

- **exercise examples:** Russian twists, medicine ball throws, or cable woodchoppers
- **functional examples:** twisting to reach behind you in the car or stirring a large pot

Gait (Walking or Running):

- **exercise examples:** treadmill walking/running, sled pushes, or stair climber
- **functional examples:** walking to work, hiking, or climbing stairs

These patterns, commonly taught in functional training, align with how our bodies are naturally designed to move.

Yoga Postures: A Path to a Healthy and Happy Body

In addition to functional movement patterns like pushing, pulling, and squatting, another powerful and time-tested way to care for the body is through the practice of yoga. The word "yoga" in Sanskrit means unification, reflecting the practice's deep focus on relationality between the Supreme Consciousness and oneself. The holistic view includes meditation, breathing techniques, philosophy, and the postures, although they serve as only one element of the broader path. The most common understanding of yoga is the application of Yoga postures, or *asanas* in Sanskrit. Asanas offer more than physical flexibility. They awaken balance, strength, breath awareness, and inner stillness. Each posture invites the body into greater alignment with the mind and spirit.

I was reminded of this during one of the most unforgettable experiences of my life—a seven-day trek through the Annapurna Trail in the Himalayan mountains of Nepal. One morning, as the mist lifted from the mountains and the sun had not yet risen, I unrolled my yoga mat with my teacher, Dada V, who taught me so much about how to have reverence for yoga practice. It didn't matter that it was a frosty morning. What mattered was moving together. Wearing heavy jackets, we remembered that yoga is not about perfect poses but about staying connected to self, to nature, and to the greater rhythm of life.

Yoga, at its core, is about connection. According to Dada V, yoga postures are a celebration of the body and a practice for cultivating a harmonious relationship with it. Through regular practice, yoga postures help remove energy blockages, fostering physical health, emotional well-being, and spiritual alignment. These blockages, or *Duhkha* (unhappiness), disrupt the natural flow of energy, creating discomfort or even disease. By restoring balance and allowing energy to move freely, yoga creates *Sukha* (happiness), ensuring that all aspects of the self—body, mind, and spirit—function in harmony.[6]

Dada V also teaches that holding a pose mindfully, synchronized with deep breathing, can quiet the mind and open the heart.

For example, standing firmly in mountain pose (*Tadasana*) while focusing on your breath invites you to feel grounded in your body and present in the moment. Over time, this intentional practice calms the nervous system, fosters emotional equilibrium, and creates a sense of sacredness in the body.

In this way, yoga postures allow you to ground in the body as your own sacred vessel. In a world that often imposes unrealistic standards on physical appearance, yoga teaches us to connect with and value our bodies for what they truly are: incredible, complex mechanisms that support us in our journey toward self-realization and unification with the Divine. As Dada V likes to say, "The human body is more remarkable than any machine you could own."[7] Through yoga postures, we can strengthen this partnership, nurturing a healthier body, a calmer mind, and a more awakened spirit. These are some of the ways Dada V claims yoga postures can benefit the body:

Strength and Flexibility. Yoga builds functional strength and flexibility, promoting better mobility and reducing the risk of injuries or strain.

Support for Joints and Bones. Strong muscles and improved alignment help stabilize joints and support the skeletal system, easing pain and preventing future problems.

Better Balance and Stability. Postures like tree pose enhance coordination and kinesthetic awareness, which are crucial as we age.

Metabolic Health. Yoga boosts metabolism by maintaining muscle tone, which helps burn calories and supports energy levels.

Holistic Integration. Yoga fosters mindfulness and connection with the body, spirit, and breath, enhancing overall physical, emotional, and spiritual well-being.

One of the greatest strengths of yoga, and yoga postures specifically, is its adaptability. They meet you where you are, whether you're recovering from an injury, managing chronic pain, or seeking deeper spiritual alignment. For example, someone with lower back pain might focus on gentle poses like Cat / Cow (*Marjaryasana / Bitilasana*) to ease tension, while someone seeking spiritual growth might emphasize meditative postures like lotus pose (*Padmasana*) combined with focused breathing techniques. Yoga postures provide accessible entry points to greater vitality, emotional peace, and a profound connection to the Divine. Their diversity shows that yoga is not a one-size-fits-all practice but a versatile path tailored to meet the unique needs of each individual.

Honoring the Body: A Lifelong Dialogue of Care and Respect

Taking care of your body is a vast and deeply personal journey, one that cannot be fully covered in a single chapter. While we've explored foundational practices such as eating nourishing foods, honoring movement, and celebrating the body through yoga postures, there are many ways to care for and connect with your body.

You might find benefits in practices like skin-care, fasting, bodywork and massage, getting regular sleep, sleep hygiene routines, mindful sexuality, or working through chronic pain and trauma stored in the body. Your body is only a machine in the sense that it requires fuel and maintenance to function properly. Truly, it is a living, evolving vessel with varied physical, emotional, and energetic needs. Therefore, taking care of your body is an act of self-respect, love, and reverence for the beautiful gift that is having a human body.

When you treat your body with the respect it deserves, you open the door to deeper mental clarity, emotional balance, and spiritual alignment. As you move forward, remember that every small step you take to honor your body brings you closer to the life you envision.

Let this chapter be the beginning of a lifelong conversation between you and your body, one built on love, listening, and care.

Weaving Together Code Four

Declaring Your Principles of Success

YOU ARE READY NOW to add on to your Higher Purpose Codex, identifying the principles of success that can be the keys to helping you accomplish your Vision Seed. But wait! Did you notice something? An earlier chapter promised "seven" secrets of success. You might wonder why we discussed only six of them in the subsequent chapters.

The story goes that when Parvatii asked Shiva this same question, Shiva replied, "'Oh Parvatii, there is no seventh factor.'"[1] I understand if this seems puzzling. Baba's explanation was simply, "If you practice these six factors, you require no seventh factor."[2]

Your Principles of Success should be practical enough to help you fulfill short-term goals but also broad enough to remind you of important mindsets and habits that allow you to find joy and peace in life. Consider this guiding question as you declare your principles: *What best practices can help me accomplish all my goals? What best practices can help me be successful in life?*

Here are some examples of strategies for success:

- delay instant gratification, so you can get something more meaningful later

- find a good mentor in the field where you want to be successful
- allow yourself to be vulnerable and to take risks
- be patient and do not rush into things
- have a steady mind
- be consistent and determined
- have an accountability buddy or join a group with a similar goal
- balance your physical, mental, and spiritual needs
- don't let limitations define you
- take care of your body

Some of these points were discussed in the previous chapters. Ultimately, it is up to you to decide what you believe will lead you to success. Use the following steps to help you write the fourth code.

Visionary Practice: Declaring Your Principles of Success

Step One: Brainstorming. Make a list of five to ten Principles of Success that are essential to helping you accomplish your goals and live a better life.

Step Two: Revisit the Higher Purpose Codex. Then, write your fourth code.

Code Four
To help my Vision Seed take root and thrive, these are my Principles of Success...

Sample

*To help my Vision Seed take root and thrive, these are
my personal Principles of Success: I will practice firm
determination, follow the wisdom of my teachers and mentors,
keep my mind steady, and always care for my body.*

Step Three: Reflecting. Write about each of your principles, and describe why they are important to you. Write what feels resonant now, knowing you can update this list as your life changes.

MILESTONE MARKER. Congratulations! If you have established your Principles of Success and added them to your Higher Purpose Codex, you have achieved the fourth milestone in our book. Celebrate big and keep the momentum going!

Part Five

Your Visionary Practices

Become a Visionary Practitioner

ONE NIGHT, I HAD A DREAM that took place in Sucre, Bolivia, the city where my grandmother was born. I was on a bus with my family members and friends. It was all familiar, yet strange. So many different figures from my life were riding on the bus with me. Then suddenly, we were at my grandmother's house. She was standing in her kitchen with wild hair sticking up, and she was speaking in a sharp, nervous way. My aunt Maria stood nearby, and my students appeared too, though it was unusual for this mix of people to be in this place.

I had a nagging feeling that I needed to wash my hair. I was feeling dirty, as if I had gone hiking all day, and felt unprepared. In the dream, my group agreed to meet at 6:30 PM to go sightseeing, but instead of getting ready, I stayed in the kitchen, catching up with my grandmother and aunt. When the time came, I felt panic. My hair still wasn't clean. I wasn't ready. I needed help. One of my mentors appeared. I wanted to pull him aside to ask for guidance, explaining why I would be late. But he wouldn't come close.

I woke up confused. I knew there was a message beneath the discomfort. So, I meditated, and I asked for the dream's meaning. *Why was my grandmother so unsettled? Why did I feel so unready?* The answer that came to me was this: my grandmother's agitation in the dream wasn't just hers. It was ancestral. It was the echo of generations who had lived with unresolved sorrow. I felt the pain that had never been laid to rest. The dirty hair, the missed appointment, the inability to get help from my teacher, were all symbols of something that needs attention and resolution. The ancestors were calling for important work to be done.

So, I listened.

That dream became a guide for a ceremony I later led for my family. We created an Andean *Despacho*, which is an elaborate offering to *Pachamama* (the Cosmic Mother) where we layered seeds, flowers, and other natural elements along with prayers. However, because of the dream, we included something more. We sent love and peace to our ancestors when they were alive. We sent healing directed to the past, so that any negativity still lingering might finally rest, and we also sent healing to family members who were currently going through distress.

Letting my dream rearrange the way I approach ceremony, family, and other aspects of our waking life is an example of a Visionary Practice. By taking action after interpreting my dream, I was not just receiving insight but responding to it. As per the teachings of my lineage, I was letting the inner world of dreams shape what I do in the physical world.

Visionary Practice is something you do to expand your vision. On a very spiritual level, these practices can expand your consciousness. Whether that happens through a conversation with a trusted guide or the repetition of a mantra during meditation, Visionary Practice is about shifting your relationship with reality. It invites you to soften the hardened places within you, to be less armored, more open, more receptive. Visionary Practices teach you to notice what is speaking, not just with words, but through symbols, sensations, and intuition.

Throughout this book, Visionary Practices were central to building and completing your Higher Purpose Codex. Having explored the Visionary Practices in this book, you now have experience as a visionary practitioner. I want to invite you to lean into that identity to help you lead wisely and see clearly.

Become a Visionary Practitioner

Visionary Practice is not reserved for mystics, monks, or people on mountaintops. It lives in boardrooms, studios, family gatherings, and on writing desks. It's practiced by world leaders and artists, educators and entrepreneurs, anyone who has slowed down to listen to something deeper than the surrounding noise. What unites them is not what they do, but how they do it: with presence, intuition, and a willingness to be guided by something greater than the surface mind. Here are three such figures whose Visionary Practices shaped not only their lives, but the culture we live in.

Oprah Winfrey: Media Personality and Icon. Oprah has long spoken about the importance of her spiritual life, which she considers central to her leadership. At the height of her career, with a schedule most would find overwhelming, she turned to Transcendental Meditation (TM) to ground herself.[1] She maintains a practice of sitting in stillness twice a day, creating space to reconnect with her center. Oprah even offered all of her employees a chance to learn TM claiming, "The results have been awesome. Better sleep. Improved relationships with spouses, children, coworkers. Some people who once suffered migraines don't anymore. Greater productivity and creativity all around."[2] She is also a bridge. Through her influence, she introduced the world to the writings of prominent visionary practitioners such as Marianne Williamson, Eckhart Tolle, and Don Miguel Ruiz.

Gloria Anzaldúa: Writer, Feminist, and Queer Theorist. Gloria Anzaldúa was not only a groundbreaking scholar. She was also a deeply intuitive visionary practitioner. Through dream journaling, ritual writing, and deep reflection on the sacred and ancestral, Anzaldúa developed a practice of entering *Nepantla*, an Indigenous *Nahuatl* concept of being in an in-between state of cultures, identities, or inner reflection.[3] Her writing process resembled a spiritual ceremony bridging the mundane with the divine and ancestral. She often described entering altered states to allow language to come "through" her, not from her. She saw herself as a conduit for stories that needed to be told—stories silenced by colonization, patriarchy, and cultural erasure. Although she was an academic scholar, her journals, filled with dreams, meditations, and spiritual self-inquiry, were a vital part of her writing process.

Steve Jobs: Tech Innovator and Icon. Though celebrated for his technological innovations at Apple Inc., Steve Jobs was also known to be a spiritual seeker. As a young man, he traveled to India and returned with a lifelong appreciation for Zen meditation and its minimalist aspects. According to Business Insider Magazine, much of the clean, minimalist features of Apple products are credited to Jobs's orientation toward Zen values of simplicity.[4] Jobs often gave colleagues and friends copies of *Autobiography of a Yogi* by Paramahansa Yogananda, a spiritual memoir that profoundly influenced him. He read it once a year, and at his memorial service, it was the one book given to every guest.[5] As an entrepreneur and visionary practitioner, Steve Jobs's approach was not just analytical but was refined through practicing meditation, having reverence for teachers like Yogananda, and principles of Zen.

Each of these figures practiced visionary exercises in a unique form: Oprah practices meditation, Anzaldúa entered ritual space through writing, and Jobs turned to Zen for creativity and insight. They remind us that Visionary Practice is a way of engaging the world from the inside out. It is how we soften, listen, and act with purpose. It requires a willingness to listen to your own breath, your dreams, your body, ancient wisdom traditions, your ancestors, the Earth and allow that listening to guide what you do.

In this part of the book, you are invited to explore a range of Visionary Practices to help you become a visionary practitioner. Ann Filemyr recommended the first four Visionary Practices in the next chapters to us during her course, The Phenomenology of Visionary Practice and the Call to Serve, in her doctoral program. The practices intersected many spiritual traditions, and Ann curated them to create a rich, inspirational experience for each of her students.

Some practices may speak to you more than others. You might be drawn to walking pilgrimages, learning to meditate, sitting with a Tarot reader, or reframing the stories you tell about your past. You may begin to see the wisdom in your own dreams or recreate yourself outside of societal labels. Whatever path you take, remember this: Visionary Practice is not something you adopt to fix yourself. It is something you enter to remember who you truly are.

Visionary Practice: Holding Space to Learn Visionary Practices Ethically

This week, set the intention to explore new Visionary Practices and to settle into your identity as a visionary practitioner, if it feels right to you. Sometimes, learning a new Visionary Practice requires an initiation from an experienced elder or practitioner. The advantage of learning from a teacher is that the teacher usually ensures that you use the practices without hurting yourself or anyone else. They teach you how to practice what you learn ethically.

Since you are walking this path with the guidance of this book and not with an elder physically in front of you, you're on your own to hold yourself accountable. This week, as you hold space for this new chapter in your life, recall Ahimsa—the practice of non-harming in action, words, and thoughts—from the Yamas and Niyamas. Make an oath from here on out to practice Ahimsa faithfully. This is important because visionary practitioners need to cultivate a moral foundation before engaging in practices that will increase their intuition and inner strength. This way, they'll never misuse their spiritual gifts.

Visit a quiet place in nature and take a flower as an offering. Speak a promise into the flower. Make an oath that you will hurt no one for as long as you engage in Visionary Practices and for as long as you live to the best of your capacity. Offer this flower to the Earth. Consider placing it under a tree, making an altar with rocks around it to embellish your intention. If you cannot get out to a natural setting, offer a mental flower with the same intention wherever you are.

Visionary Practice

Going on Sacred Journeys

WHEN I WAS SIXTEEN, I WAS A HIGH SCHOOL JUNIOR at Annandale High School in Northern Virginia. One of my history teachers often encouraged us to visit Shenandoah National Park. At the time, I didn't really know what a national park was. But one weekend, something inside me stirred to take my teacher's recommendation. So, I got in my mother's car and drove two hours west, alone, not knowing what I'd find or what I was supposed to do once I got there.

I arrived and parked near a small stream and brought out my guitar. Back then, I was a songwriter, and without planning to, I started to write a song. The song flowed out of me, and I would call it The Drive and the Show, honoring the two-hour drive I had done that day. It is probably one of the best songs I have ever written. That day, something in the land, the water, the solitude inspired me. I felt the universe had rewarded me for saying yes to something I didn't fully understand but somehow felt was meaningful. I wouldn't have called it a pilgrimage at the time, but looking back, that was my first pilgrimage. It was my first glimpse into understanding how a journey can be a teacher and how a place can transform you.

In many Indigenous traditions, particularly among the Quechua, this act of journeying into nature with intention is known as

Willka Puriy, meaning "the sacred journey of energy." It is understood to be both an inner and outer journey, where the land itself serves as a teacher and healer. From ancient times through the present day, the Quechua make sacred treks from the city of Qosqo (Cusco) in Peru along paths that connect them to sacred temples, lagoons, and Apus (mountain guardians). Pilgrimage is a way to purify their minds, bodies, and hearts.

Embarking on a Sacred Journey

What makes a pilgrimage sacred is intention. According to *Tukuy T'ikray: The Path of Conscious Transformation for the Cosmic Being* (2019), a book co-written by my teacher Tupac T'ito Kuntur and his brother Inka T'ito Kuntur Q'osñipa, the journey begins long before your feet meet the path. It begins with the idea and preparation, when you set the intention. See if there is a question you would like to answer.

In the Andean tradition, two core principles guide a sacred journey. First, physical movement serves as detoxification: walking, climbing, and sitting with the land helps release toxins and emotional and spiritual blockages, allowing energy to move and transform. Second, places in nature are alive. Mountains, rivers, forests, deserts, and lakes are not simply scenery. They are what I call Biome Beings, conscious, natural presences that witness, protect, and guide. A pilgrimage is a way of entering into a relationship with them, offering your respect and opening yourself to receive their wisdom.

In Tupac's book *Tukuy T'ikray* (2019), he prescribes the following steps for carrying out a pilgrimage:

1. Identify or visualize the path or destination of the pilgrimage. Choose where you want to go.
2. Plan to go alone, having informed a loved one of where you will be for safety, or only with friends who share your in-

tention and respect for the experience. Going with people who are overly talkative, distracted, or not aligned with the sacredness of the experience will block your own intentions.

3. Be aware of your dreams and visions that may manifest before your pilgrimage, as they will guide your entire process.

4. Release yourself from all distractions, both internal and external. This means leaving behind negative thoughts and doubts and overcoming any weakness that may prevent you from engaging in this practice.

5. Free yourself from the electronics and conveniences of city life. Be open to experiencing non-air-conditioned rooms, cold showers, and non-readily available bathrooms if necessary. Though you may bring a phone to take photos, avoid checking email, scrolling through social media, or engaging with digital noise.

6. Bring sacred materials as offerings to the Biome Beings along the path such as beautiful flowers that you may offer to a mountain or a river, a musical instrument to produce sounds and melodies for the local environment, or sacred objects that always accompany you such as a necklace for protection, a cushion for meditation, or scented oils for relaxation.

7. Before starting, perform a ceremony to ask permission and connect with the energies and spiritual beings of the spaces you are about to visit. You can do this by facing east, south, west, or north, depending on your destination's direction, and send a greeting from your heart.

8. Walk mindfully, disconnecting from the city and all distractions. This is the time to focus your attention and connection on the sacred energies of the spaces you are entering.[1]

If your pilgrimage is not to a place in nature, that is okay. Some people may choose to go on an urban pilgrimage, such as to a historical landmark or a museum with special significance. Many of the guidelines above can still apply. As you walk your sacred path, know that not all moments will feel serene. It is normal to encounter negative desires, strange thoughts, or unsettling feelings. This is part of the emotional detox one undergoes while on pilgrimage. There may also be adverse physical reactions that are a part of the purification process, such as headaches, stomach pain, or body aches. Do not fear these reactions.

In the book *Tukuy T'ikray*, my teacher recommends turning to the spiritual guardians of the land. Call upon the Apus (mountain guardians), the rivers, the trees, Mother Earth herself to ask for guidance. Ask for healing. Offer prayers and respect. At the same time, don't hesitate to support yourself in practical ways: bring bug spray, altitude medicine, or anything that offers gentle relief. Caring for your body and spirit goes hand in hand on this sacred journey.

Reaching Your Destination

If your goal is to reach a sacred mountain, temple, or place that you felt called to visit, trust that it holds the secret to your healing and transformation. Upon arrival, practice what the Quechua call *Thaq Kay* (a state of stillness and calming of the body's energy). Lie down on the ground, close your eyes, and breathe deeply. Enter a sacred state where the energies and beings of the local natural place can assist your healing. Remain in this state for at least 30 minutes or longer. During this time, you can also do meditation or any of your spiritual practices that place you into a pure state of consciousness.

Close by digging a small hole representing the source of cosmic energy. Place a natural offering there, such as seeds or delicious foods that you brought with you as snacks. Invoke your gratitude, saying "thank you" three times to the land and the sacred beings who received you. This is a moment to express heartfelt gratitude, sealing the transformation and purification you have experienced.

After the pilgrimage, carry the clarity, purity, and connection you have gained back into your daily life. See if the question you may have asked at the beginning has been answered. Write about your experience and share what you learned with a friend.

Reframing the Stories We Tell About Ourselves

THE STORIES WE TELL about the challenges we've lived through can become a wound or a cage. They shape how we look to the future, and they live in our bodies and beliefs as failures, traumas, or missed opportunities. What matters is not only what happened but how we carry it. It takes skill to examine our stories and find hidden gifts and powers, if we know how to use them.

For example, at seventeen-years-old, Veronica was in a devastating car accident. She wasn't driving, but she was the only one after the accident who was flown to the hospital in a helicopter. A fractured spine left her in recovery for nearly a year, relearning how to move and trust her body again. For a long time, her story was simple: *Everything changed that day. My youth was stolen. I missed out on senior year.* And that version was true. No one could deny the amount of pain she went through. But over time, other versions spoke.

In one version, she saw herself as a survivor, someone who had touched death and had come back wiser. The accident had slowed her down enough to begin listening inward. In another version, thanks to the accident, she rediscovered her faith, something she had ignored in the rush of adolescence. A third version allowed her to appreciate how her family had come together in a way they hadn't before. She imagined the story from the perspective of her best friend Maria, who was driving, and who'd always felt guilty for asking Veronica to come along that day.

Each version told a different truth. In time, Veronica gave space for each of them to exist. Her mother offered her a book with a quote inside by Oprah Winfrey—"Turn your wounds into wisdom"— it said, and it inspired her to grow. Her story became a wellspring of resilience rather than a fixed scar. The event hadn't changed. What changed was how she carried it, which allowed her to heal.

Like Veronica, you may discover that a major, challenging event in your life can hold many truths: some painful, some empowering, and some still unfolding. Practicing this kind of reframing helps to transform the storyteller. As you retell your own story from different angles, you'll see yourself not just as the one who was hurt but also as the one who grew, the one who witnessed, and the one who learned. This process helps loosen the grip of disempowering narratives and makes room for new insights to emerge.

How to Practice Reframing

First, choose a personal story. This story should be something emotionally significant, unresolved, or still shaping your inner narrative. Write the story five different ways. Begin with the wounded—from the place of loss or suffering. Then, tell it from different angles offered here or from other perspectives:

The Wounded. Start here. Write what happened from your initial impression or understanding. Tell the story from a place of pain or loss. Write about what hurt or what felt unfair.

The Survivor. Tell it from the perspective of someone who made it through. Write what helped you survive and what strength you found.

The Hero/Shero. Tell the story from a place of triumph. How did you rise above? What did you gain? How were you transformed?

The Learner. Tell the story focusing on what you learned. What new meaning does the experience carry?

The Witness. Tell the story from a higher or more spiritual perspective. What was the soul lesson? What did others in the story learn, too?

The Other People. Tell the story from another person's perspective who was involved in the situation. Put yourself in their shoes and write it from their point of view. What made them choose what they did? What was in their best interest? What did they learn?

The Fly on the Wall. Tell the story from a completely neutral perspective. How would a fly on the wall observe everything that was happening in the situation? From a neutral perspective, describe the behavior of everyone involved.

The Future Me. Tell the story as though it were five to ten years in the future. What matters now? Imagine the steps you took to heal. Try telling the story from a future version of yourself who is at peace.

After you've written all five (or more) versions, pause and reflect. Which one surprised you? Which one felt liberating? What shifts when you allow more than one version to be true? The practice of rewriting a story five different ways is not about pretending that harm didn't happen or that suffering doesn't matter. Instead, this practice allows us to heal by giving us full agency to transform our challenges into lessons.

Asserting Your Archetypal Identity

DURING ONE OF OUR MANY DISCUSSIONS on fulfilling our Vision Seeds and the obstacles we face, Ann Filemyr once explained:

> We are not free from the society we live in. We live inside systems that define categories of personhood by gender, race, age, ability, and more. These definitions are encoded in laws, policies, and cultural norms. But at the same time, we can assert an inner identity. One that may not be visible to others but is deeply known within us.[1]

You are invited to examine two dimensions of yourself in this Visionary Practice. First, your intersectional identity—the overlapping categories of identity you carry such as race, gender, class, and sexuality and how they interact to shape your unique experiences of oppression and privilege.[2] Then, name your archetypal identity—a deeper understanding of the self, rooted in inner knowing and symbolism. By naming your archetypal identity in this chapter, you will give yourself permission to name the inner force that guides you, even when it defies social definitions.

Asserting Your Archetypal Identity

Archetypes appear in many cultures and spiritual traditions, from trickster figures in Indigenous stories to wise elders in folktales or from the Greek goddess Athena to the High Priestess Major Archana card in Tarot cards. These shared symbols give us a language to express examples of strength, creativity, resilience, or transformation.

The archetype we resonate with may not necessarily fit with how other people perceive us. For example, a person labeled by society as a woman might feel boxed in by expectations to be nurturing, accommodating, or submissive. Yet when she reflects inwardly, she sees something different and claims: *I am a warrior*. Another person might be seen as a blue-collar worker, but within, they feel more like a mystic, a forest fairy, or a shape-shifter. Archetypal identity is where your essence speaks. It opens space for vision and fluidity. It may also reveal your inner power or gifts. See if any of the following archetypal identities matches how you feel on the inside:

Table 1

Archetypal Identities - Priestess

queen / king	shaman	crone
goddess	priest / priestess	artist
mother / father	monk / nun	healer
warrior	angel	freedom fighter
hermit	messiah	trickster
lover	samaritan / altruist	jester
witch	mentor	child

As you explore your own archetypal identity, you are welcome to consider an established archetype named in the table above or from another culture around the world that resonates with you. Do this with respect, offering credit where credit is due. You may also imagine a new one that feels true to your core. What matters most is that the archetype you choose reflects the deeper energy and wisdom you carry within. Follow the steps below to get started.

Step One: Acknowledge Your Intersectional Identity. First, get clear with how society sees you on the outside. In life, one of our challenges is to strike a balance between what society imposes on our personhood and who we feel we are on the inside. Find a quiet space and take time to reflect on the following:

- How has society defined you?
- What labels have been placed on you because of your race, gender, sexuality, age, class, nationality, language, or physical ability? Create a full list or an intersectional identity wheel.
- Which of these labels has created opportunities or challenges in your life?
- Which feel accurate or positive? Which feel limiting, painful, or untrue?

Step Two: Name Your Archetypal Identity. Now shift your focus inward. Close your eyes, breathe, and let go of who you've been told to be. Ask yourself:

- Who do you feel you truly are at the symbolic or inner level?
- If you could describe your essence or your inner truth, what image or archetype arises? Are you a healer, a phoenix, a protector, a wanderer, or a sage?
- What energy or archetypal figure mirrors who you know yourself to be?

Step Three: Illustrate Your Archetypal Identity. After you write your reflections, draw or create a collage of your archetypal identity with multiple images. Allow yourself to name and claim your archetypal truth, even if no one else sees it yet. Keep this portrait close to remind you of your inner strength.

After completing this Visionary Practice, walk with the awareness of who you are beyond society's labels. Observe any feelings of liberation or empowerment you might have gained. Keep the image you created in a visible place to remind you of your higher self on days you feel low.

Consulting an Oracle for Guidance

WHETHER THE PATH TO ACCOMPLISHING your Vision Seed feels clear or not, it can be deeply insightful to consult an oracle on how this journey may unfold from a purely intuitive perspective. Across cultures and centuries, oracles have served as sacred messengers, those who help us see beyond the veil of everyday perception. In ancient Greece, there was a priestess known as the Oracle of Delphi, who entered a trance to receive divine messages from the god Apollo. In West Africa, the Ifá diviners cast sacred objects and interpret their patterns, speaking on behalf of Orisha deities and ancestral spirits. Spiritual seekers have long used divination tools like cards, symbols, stones, leaves, shells, and intuitive messages to find patterns, name hidden forces, and receive insight.

Although most people in fortune-telling or divination sessions are interested in knowing the future, that does not have to be your objective. These sessions can also be very helpful in simply illuminating what lies beneath the surface. Here are some examples of divination practices you may find in different regions and cultures:

Tarot and Oracle Card Readers. Tarot uses a deck of symbolic images to reflect your inner state and help reveal potential paths.

Coca Leaf Readers (Andes). In Andean traditions, coca leaves are placed on a sacred cloth and read for patterns by a trained spiritual reader, offering insight into the present, future, and hidden energies at play.

Shell Diviners (Africa and Caribbean). In traditions such as Ifá, shells are cast to receive guidance from the Orishas or ancestral spirits.

Runes and I Ching. These are ancient symbolic systems that can be cast or selected to offer archetypal wisdom and decision-making clarity.

Today, the oracular tradition continues. Though the oracles of our modern times may sit at a Tarot table, they still hold a sacred role. They help us attune to what is emerging and receive messages from Spirit or the subconscious that may otherwise remain hidden.

I invite you to give yourself the opportunity to visit a local oracle or psychic. This may be a Tarot reader in your neighborhood or perhaps a friend whom you trust to have an intuitive gift and a method for giving you information. What matters most is not the form but the quality of intention and the clarity of the question you bring. You might ask questions such as, "What do I need to know about my Vision Seed now to help me accomplish it? What must I release to move forward with clarity? What is supporting or obstructing the growth of my vision?"

How to Choose Your Oracle

While the world of oracles is rich and varied, whom you choose to consult matters. Ideally, the person you sit with should be recommended by someone you trust. The person making the recommendation should be someone who had a positive, respectful, and insightful experience with the reader. When we open ourselves to spiritual guidance, especially in vulnerable moments, it is important to do so in safe company. Your reader should be kind and appear to genuinely care for your well-being. They should communicate clearly and behave ethically.

Avoid readers who offer grandiose guarantees or stir up fear to upsell unnecessary services. Some may suggest a follow-up purification session, energy work, or a ritual to help you integrate the reading or fulfill your objective. This is not inherently a red flag, and sometimes can be helpful. But remember, you are never obligated. Only say yes to additional work if it genuinely resonates and aligns with your own intuition and needs. At its core, a reading is not about handing your power over to someone else. It is about helping you tap into your own intuition with the help of a trusted reader.

Remember that no oracle seals your fate. What they offer is not a fixed destiny but rather a map of potential paths. These paths can shift, deepen, or dissolve based on your actions and choices.

Be open and not overly concerned with testing the reader's psychic powers. Help the reader help you by providing the necessary information they need to give you insight. Focus on getting the most information on your topic possible, especially any areas that seem unclear. However, rely on specialists to give you important information. Don't go to the Tarot reader for financial advice, instead speak to a financial professional.

Even if you are skeptical of an oracle's ability to foresee the future, the experience can still hold value. Many oracular systems, such as the Tarot, are built on rich archetypes and symbols that speak to the human experience. These images can act like mirrors, reflecting hidden aspects of your own thoughts, emotions, and possibilities. In this way, a reading can function less as fortune-telling and more as a creative brainstorming, a way of exploring new perspectives on your challenges and opportunities.

You may find that the symbols spark your imagination, deepen your reflection, or uncover ideas you hadn't considered. Think of it as a tool for thinking outside of the box or probing with the language of symbols or archetypes. Whether or not you take the reading literally, what matters most is uncovering fresh perspectives that can move your project forward.

Integrating Your Reading After the Session

One of the best outcomes that can emerge after your reading is a feeling of clarity and positivity. Once your session concludes, take the time to:

- sit quietly
- write what resonated and what felt off
- write what new insights emerged

Pay close attention to what follows because guidance from an oracle is a doorway, not a destination. Dreams may reveal insights. Symbols in the reading may repeat. People may appear with timely advice. Your task becomes tracking what unfolds.

See if the reading stirred a forgotten truth, unblocked a creative impulse, or brought a shadow into the light. Be curious. Be patient. But above all, stay rooted in your own sense of sovereignty and discernment. Oracles help us refocus, clarify, and reconnect with what's most essential. But they do not replace your own wisdom. They are simply another voice for Spirit to guide your path, reminding you that you are not alone, and that guidance is always available if you know how to ask and how to listen.

Developing Kinship with an Animal or Biome Guide

IN NATIVE AMERICAN TRADITIONS, especially among the Anishinaabeg (Ojibwe/Chippewa, Potawatomi, and Ottawa/Odawa) of North America and the Quechua of South America, humans are not separate from nature. We are part of a sacred web including people, animals, plants, rivers, mountains, and unseen spiritual forces. To live in balance within this system is to acknowledge that more-than-human relatives such as animals, rivers, mountains, and trees are not "resources" or background scenery. They are kinship alliances, teachers, and guides.

Within the Ojibwe tradition, this understanding takes form in the *Dodaim* (often anglicized as "totem") system, a powerful spiritual and social structure of animal clans that shapes a person's identity, community role, and sacred responsibility. As described in *Ojibwe Waasa Inaabidaa: We look in all directions* (2002) by Thomas Peacock and Marlene Wisuri, the Dodaim system originated when five animals emerged from the ocean and came to live among the Ojibwe people. These beings became the ancestors of the original animal clans.

Dodaims were passed down through the father's line, and each clan held specific gifts and responsibilities:

- Crane, loon, goose, eagle, and hawk clans are related to leadership roles.
- Bear, wolf, and lynx clans are related to roles of defense and protection.
- Deer, moose, beaver, and muskrat clans provided sustenance.
- Sturgeon, catfish, sucker, and whitefish denoted teaching and learning.
- Turtle, otter, snake, frog, and water being clans provided medicine.[1]

To belong to a Dodaim is to know your purpose and your role in the community. These animal guides are inherited, and they shape how one moves through the world.

Ann Filemyr was herself a student of this path. In her early years, Ann apprenticed with an Anishinaabeg (Ojibwe) elder named Keewaydinoquay, affectionately known to her students as Grandmother Kee. Through Grandmother Kee's guidance, Ann was taught the songs, stories, ceremonies, and kinship teachings that rooted her in Anishinaabeg lifeways. Ann would eventually become a teacher in Grandmother Kee's lineage, carrying and sharing what had been entrusted to her.

Years later, Ann shared with me lessons rooted in the teachings of Grandmother Kee. One of my assignments was to search for the animal clan, or Dodaim, that I belonged to. I would take on this quest during one of my pilgrimages to Peru. Ann invited me to seek an ancient kin, a guide that could walk beside me spiritually as I stepped into deeper learning.

Kinship With an Animal Guide

I set my intention to meet my Dodaim by paying attention to dreams and synchronicities. At first, I saw dogs appear and thought perhaps they were my guides. But over time, through more dreams, insights, and consultation with my Quechua elders, I received a deeper confirmation: my Dodaim was not the dog but the condor.

In Quechua cosmology, the condor is sacred. It flies at the highest altitudes, representing the Celestial World (*Hanan Pacha*), which is the realm of spirit, ancestors, and divine clarity. My Dodaim guides how I live. The condor is not a predator. It feeds on what is already dead, cleansing the Earth of decay and restoring balance to the ecosystem. This reminds me to be regenerative, to transmute what is no longer useful in my life and to contribute to the healing of what has been cast aside.

Condors are selective about what they eat. They search for specific organs within a carcass to nourish themselves first. This reminds me to be intentional and discerning, especially about what I consume, whether food, information, or who I spend time with.

Condors also lay a single egg per year, and both parents take turns incubating it with devoted care. This teaches me about the value of focused parenting and giving my children my full presence and shared responsibility with their mother. For me, kinship with an animal guide has been empowering in practical and esoteric ways. Through this sacred relationship, I draw real inspiration and direction.

Kinship With a Biome Being

As I began the work of meeting my Dodaim in the Andes Mountains of Peru, I learned something important from the Quechua paqos (shamans) I was studying with—in Andean cosmology, the primary guides are often not animals, but mountain guardians known as Apus. While animal guides offer companionship and wisdom from the world of creatures, the Quechua Andean tradition reminds us that deep relationships can also occur with land features or places.

In Quechua cosmology, each person is born into the care of an Apu or *Ñusta Apu* (female mountain guardian). Female mountains are usually distinguished by having round tops as opposed to pointy mountain peaks associated with masculine mountains. According to the paqos, if near your birth there were no mountains, your guardian could be another type of Biome Being, such as a river, a volcano, a waterfall, or another natural feature of the Earth. These beings are living entities with presence, consciousness, and purpose. They have watched you from birth and can be an important guide in your life.

According to the Quechua, an Apu receives you at birth like a guardian angel, witnessing your very first breath. While most people do not remember this connection consciously, the Apu remembers. So, it is never too late to deepen that relationship.

Biome Beings can be invoked in daily life for strength, for insight, or simply for grounding. For example, Quechua paqos invoke their benefactor Apu when performing a healing ceremony, so the Apu can give power to the healing. Many engage formally through ceremony and pilgrimage, bringing offerings such as coca leaves, flowers, or other acts of reverence to the being itself. To stand in the presence of your Apu or to sit beside your guiding river is to remember that you are not alone. You are held, seen, and known by something vast and deeply rooted.

A Note on the Decolonial Nature of This Work

For many, this journey to discover an animal or biome guide is more than a personal or spiritual quest. It can also be a profound act of decolonization. Since the onset of colonialism in the Americas, Europeans systematically dismissed, suppressed, or erased Indigenous knowledge systems. Therefore, seeking guidance through Indigenous ways of knowing means confronting the ongoing colonial legacy of cultural erasure and occupation regardless of your cultural background.

Engaging in a Visionary Practice, rooted in Indigenous ways, must be approached with care, humility, and respect. This is not about claiming an Indigenous identity that is not yours. Rather, it is about openness and reverence for the Indigenous worldview you are exploring. This can be done respectfully when you honor the specific cultural roots these practices come from.

Begin the Journey to Your Animal or Biome Being Guide

When exploring the path to discovering your Biome Being guide, it is important to move with care and respect. For the best results, seek the guidance of an experienced teacher or elder who can walk with you through the process. Always acknowledge the cultural source of the teachings you receive and give credit where it is due. Rather than approaching these practices with a mindset of ownership, come intending to build relationships. Let your steps be guided by reverence, ethics, and respect.

If you feel called to discover your own Apu or Biome Being with the support of an experienced elder, I invite you to reach out to me through my contact page at www.gustavomonje.com.

Practicing Meditation:
The Inner Pilgrimage

OF ALL THE VISIONARY PRACTICES available to us, meditation is both ancient and widely practiced. Across cultures and lineages, sitting in stillness, closing our eyes, turning inward, and allowing our minds to settle are practices of deep listening and homecoming.

In the ancient yogic tradition of India, meditation is not simply a tool for relaxation. It is a pathway to Brahma, the Supreme Consciousness of the universe. However, there are many ways to meditate. Different practices serve different purposes. The key is to understand your needs. Some people meditate to regulate emotions, reduce anxiety, or build focus. These are important and valid goals, especially in today's stress-filled world. Others meditate for spiritual insight, mystical connection, or the desire to awaken their higher self.

Here are a few forms of meditation to explore:

Mindfulness Meditation. Mindfulness is common in Buddhist traditions and secular wellness groups. Mindfulness meditation involves observing one's thoughts, breath, or sensations without judgment. It builds awareness and emotional balance. It can be the best option for someone who is not necessarily seeking spirituality.

Loving-Kindness (*Metta*) Meditation. Metta is a heart-centered Buddhist practice that cultivates compassion and forgiveness toward oneself and others. It is ideal for softening inner criticism, overcoming jealousy, and fostering sympathetic joy toward others.

Breath Meditation (Pranayama). Breathwork uses conscious breathing techniques to regulate energy, calm the nervous system, and open subtle channels. It can also be positioned as a secular practice.

Mantra Meditation. This type of meditation uses the silent repetition of a sacred sound, word, or phrase to calm the mind or connect with the Divine. It helps focus the heart, deepen devotion, and bring the soul closer to its Source. Depending on the school, mantra meditation can be deeply spiritual or secular.

Devotional or *Bhakti* Chanting. Singing mantras rather than reciting them silently is also a meditative practice. There are many sacred mantras to sing *Kirtan*. Kirtan is the practice of devotional chanting or singing. Chanting or singing mantras with friends can generate a powerful transformative vibration. The key here is to chant with love for experiencing the highest bliss.

There are many more types of meditations than are mentioned here. Each form opens a different doorway and a different inner journey. In addition, meditation can get more complex when you incorporate the visualization of chakras or other psychic elements in the subtle body, creating a more profound inner pilgrimage. What matters most is knowing why you are going on the journey.

Before choosing a practice, ask yourself: Am I meditating simply to calm my emotions? Do I seek spiritual union and connection with the Divine? Once you're clear on your purpose, seek a practice or a teacher that aligns with it. Let your intention guide your exploration.

Using Astrology as a Tool
for Self-Knowledge

"YOU'RE A LEO, SO YOU'RE EGOTISTICAL." "You're a Pisces, so you must be sensitive." Astrology is one of the most ancient and widespread systems of wisdom known to humanity. However, it is often misunderstood and reduced to clichés.

While it is common to associate Astrology with generic horoscopes found in magazines, when practiced with depth, it can be a fun tool for self-knowledge. The key is to look beyond the sign attributed to your birthday. Equally important, Astrology offers a framework for understanding others. Studying other people's birth charts can bring compassion and clarity to familial relationships, support you in seeing compatibility with romantic partners, and help you better appreciate the nature of the surrounding people. In this way, Astrology is not just about predicting the future; it is about building a deeper awareness of yourself and those you share your life with.

You can use Astrology to develop kinship with our solar system's planets—the Moon, Venus, Saturn, or Jupiter. These are not just distant abstract orbs circling in space. Across time, they have watched over us, carrying gravitational and symbolic influence. Through Astrological study and reverent attention, we recognize them not only as celestial bodies but as spiritual allies. This understanding invites us to honor the sky not as a backdrop, but as a living field of connection and guidance.

A full Astrological birth chart is a detailed map of the sky at the moment and location of your birth. It shows the exact positions of the planets, the constellations they occupy, and how those arrangements reflect patterns of behavior, insight, and potential in your life. People around the world practice many systems of Astrology. Tropical Astrology is the most common Western system, based on the solar calendar and seasonal cycles. Sidereal Astrology, often linked with Vedic or *Jyotish* Astrology, aligns more closely with the actual constellations in the sky.

Vedic Astrology

Each system offers something meaningful, but I follow Vedic Astrology for its depth and perceived precision. Rooted in ancient scriptures, Vedic Astrology or *Jyotish*, meaning science of light, uses the sidereal zodiac and provides insights into both planetary positions and star constellations called *Nakshatras*, which provide additional layers of knowledge.

A full Vedic birth chart offers a comprehensive look at your life path and personality. As in Tropical Astrology, the chart includes 12 houses, each reflecting a different domain of life, such as:

- **1st House:** personality, self-image, and physical presence
- **4th House:** home life, emotional security, relationship with the mother
- **7th House:** partnerships, marriage, relating to others
- **10th House:** career, public life, and legacy
- **12th House:** spiritual life, isolated places, and travel overseas

In Vedic astrology, your chart reveals not only the planetary placements in zodiac signs but also their positions within Nakshatras, lunar constellations that also influence your personality. Understanding Nakshatras can answer questions like: What drives me? What karma am I working with? The Nakshatra of your Moon, in particular, can offer deep insight into your emotional temperament, instincts, and subconscious tendencies.

Beyond the main birth chart, Vedic Astrology also includes a system of divisional charts, or *Vargas*, which provide focused views into specific areas of life. What might your partnerships teach you as you mature? How does your life look after age 36? The ninth divisional chart (D9), called *Navamsha*, speaks to your married life and your life in later years. These additional layers reveal how commitment, wisdom, and your planetary placements mature as you grow.

You may also explore *Mahadasha* periods, which are planetary time cycles, of six years or in some cases 18 years, that can answer questions like: What is the overall theme or "climate" of my current life phase? When are major life events likely to occur? These cycles can help you observe prevalent themes emerging in different eras of your life. Keep in mind that Astrology should never limit or define you but rather bring clarity and a deeper sense of timing.

We are naturally curious about who we are, and a Vedic birth chart serves as a mirror, reflecting your strengths, challenges, and the many dimensions of our life. Each house on the chart opens a window into different areas of experience—identity, family, relationships, career, and spirituality—helping you see how these parts interconnect.

How to Get Started

To begin, you will need your exact date, time, and location of birth. You will also need a reliable Vedic Astrology website or software such as Cosmic Insights to generate your chart. From there, you can consult a trusted astrologer to read your chart. Ideally, this should be someone recommended by a friend or whose work you've vetted for integrity and accuracy.

You can also learn how to interpret your own chart. Many gifted astrologers now share free teachings on YouTube. Once you know your placements, you can search for videos like "Moon in Rohini Nakshatra" or "Mars in the 10th House." Take notes on what your planetary placements mean, explore various interpretations, and see what resonates.

Final Cautionary Note

As may be the case with visiting an oracle or using Astrology for predictions, you never want to feel bound in any fatalistic way to their guidance. Trust in your own lived experience and do not become dependent on any one tool of divination to make all your decisions. If you have a good idea or a good plan, always follow that without hesitation. Astrology is meant to assist you. It should never instill fear or restrict you.

Weaving Together Code Five

Expanding Through Visionary Practices

"Being a Jedi is not just about power, or lightsabers, or even skill with the Force. It is about connection. Being part of something bigger."
—*Obi-Wan Kenobi. Charles Soule, Star Wars: Obi-Wan & Anakin*

AS YOU WALK THE PATH OF YOUR VISION SEED, remember that clarity does not always arrive through personal will alone. Your life in enriched when you create openness and space for inspiration to arrive from unexpected places. Visionary Practices create that space. Whether you are meditating on a mantra, uncovering your archetypal identity, consulting an oracle, discovering your animal or biome kin, or walking a sacred pilgrimage, each practice helps you see yourself and your path from a new angle. These experiences humble the ego and tap into the soul. As you continue forward, allow these sacred practices to support you. Let them whisper reminders of who you truly are and where your spirit longs to go.

In the previous chapters, you explored a range of Visionary Practices. Now it's time to return to your Higher Purpose Codex. You've already named your purpose, values, Vision Seed, and Principles of Success. Here, you will add your fifth code: your intended engagement with Visionary Practices. Remember to always ground your spiritual development in your core values to help you expand with integrity.

Visionary Practice: Expanding with Visionary Practices

Step One: Brainstorming. Make a list of Visionary Practices you feel called to practice regularly. What practices can best help you expand your mind, heart, and intuition?

Step Two: Revisit the Higher Purpose Codex. Then, write your fifth code.

Code Five
To expand mentally and spiritually, I will engage with the following Visionary Practices...

Sample
To expand mentally and spiritually, I will engage with the following Visionary Practices: practice meditation and daily grounding rituals, foster kinship alliances with more-than-human beings, read astrological charts to know myself and others better, journey to sacred places to learn and heal from place-fields.

Step Three: Reflecting. Write a paragraph about each of the practices you have chosen and why they are important to you. Write what feels resonant now, knowing you can update this list as your spiritual life grows.

MILESTONE MARKER: Take a moment to acknowledge how far you've come. By completing this section, you've reached the fifth milestone of the book! You're not just thinking about transformation. You are actively cultivating it as visionary practitioner! After you have amended your codex with the fifth code, celebrate. Call for a pizza or simply lie out under the stars to reflect on your becoming.

Part Six

Your Visionary Action Plan

Invitation

Map the Path Ahead with Visionary Tools

THANK YOU FOR MAKING IT THIS FAR! You've come a long way in your Higher Purpose Codex. You planted a Vision Seed and are now taking the next steps to seeing it bloom.

Remember, planting the Vision Seed alone will not manifest what you are seeking. The world is full of beautiful dreams left unlived. Many times, dreams are left unlived because they were never given a structure to hold them. This last part of the book is about follow-through, and not just the "doing," but the conscious tending of your dream. As you move into the planning and action phase, remember the proper outlook is not working toward perfection. Rather, a safer route is acting with devotion, returning again and again to what matters, even when doubt, fear, or fatigue tries to pull you off course.

But before we dive into tools and timelines, let us draw upon an ancient symbolic framework that has guided seekers, mystics, and visionaries for centuries: the Tarot. Far from being just a deck of fortune-telling cards, the Tarot is a mythic map of the soul's journey through life, transformation, and purpose. Rooted in medieval Europe but shaped by far older symbolic traditions including Egyptian mysticism, numerology, astrology, Kabbalah, and archetypal psychology, the Tarot reflects a universal language of growth and change.[1] It is a visual framework offering a comprehensive look for any Vision Seed project.

Four Realms of Your Vision Seed

A core component of the Tarot is the four suits of the Minor Arcana: Swords, Cups, Wands, and Pentacles. In Rachel Pollack's (2019) book *Seventy-Eight Degrees of Wisdom: A Tarot Journey to Self-Awareness*, considered an authoritative text by many Tarot practitioners, she argues that each suit of the Minor Archana "as a whole show activities and qualities of life."

In a Tarot reading, a seeker may gain answers to their question by pulling a Minor Archana card and receive insight that may connect with using your intellect (Swords), reflecting on your emotions (Cups), diving into a situation with passion (Wands) or tending to physical needs (the Pentacles). These suits correspond to the four natural elements. Just as air, water, fire, and earth are elements necessary for life, so too can the suits symbolize essential dimensions of your project. I invite you to consider how each suit can represent a different dimension of your Vision Seed process:

- **Swords (air)** invite you to sharpen your clarity and cut through illusion.
- **Cups (water)** invite you to feel and open your heart.
- **Wands (fire)** ignite your will.
- **Pentacles (Earth)** ground you.

I offer this framework not as a system for divination in this case, but as a symbolic structure to support your action plan. When you feel scattered, unsure, or overwhelmed, the concepts and questions related to these archetypes can reorient you. Some days, you'll need the sharp logic of the Swords to cut through distraction. Other days will call for the boldness of Wands, the heart of Cups, or the grounded follow-through of Pentacles. As you move forward into the practical work of project design and execution, use the four Minor Arcana suits as a compass, a check-in, or even as a tool for analysis.

Swords: The Realm of Intellect and Clarity

Swords remind you that ideas need to be sharpened. They teach you the importance of clarity, honesty, and intention. But beware. Over-thinking or harsh self-judgment can cut your efforts short. Use this energy to clarify—not critique—your vision.

Key Concepts. ideas, strategy, discernment, communication, technology, decision-making, conflicts, boundaries, discernment.

Over-Arching Question. What mindset am I bringing to my Vision Seed?

Related Questions.
- Is my Vision Seed clear?
- What do I need to learn or understand?
- What technical skills do I possess or need to acquire?
- What digital, physical, or other tools can I utilize to carry out my Vision Seed?
- What are the possible setbacks or conflicts I may face?
- What are the risks to myself or others involved in my project?
- Do I have a growth mindset or a fixed mindset?

Cautionary Reminder. Have I lost clarity?

Cups – The Realm of Emotion and Connection

Cups guide your "why," the heartfelt motivation behind your vision. Without a deep well of emotional meaning, projects can become hollow or draining. Cups teach you to receive, feel, and trust. They also remind you to care for your emotional body, rest when needed, and return to the sacred when things feel dry or forced.

Key Concepts. compassion, dreams, empathy, inner-alignment, heart-centeredness, spirituality, emotional resonance, joy.

Over-Arching Question. Am I staying connected to my why?

Related Questions.
- Does this vision feel true to my Higher Purpose?
- What emotional healing must happen
  for me to move forward?
- Are there limiting beliefs that I need to heal to advance?
- How can I stay connected to love and empathy—
  for myself and others—during this journey?
- What Visionary Practices will I do to stay
  inspired or as part of my self-care plan?
- Am I paying attention to dreams or visions
  that can guide my path forward?

Cautionary Reminder. Have I lost heart?

Wands: The Realm of Passion and Action

Wands are the ignition—the spark that propels you from dreaming to doing. They give you the courage to start, to face fear, to move even when the outcome isn't clear. They remind of your what you stand to gain and who is in your network for support. They carry the grounded and creative energy of the Earth. With Wands energy, you branch out and move forward with decisions.

Key Concepts. creativity, drive, courage, willpower, energetic movement, joy, excitement, motivation, business.

Over-Arching Question. Am I taking action?

Related Questions.
- What lights me up about my Vision Seed?
- Where do I feel called to act boldly?
- How can I take risks in service of this vision?
- What is my wildest dream related to my Vision Seed?
- How can I make my work fun?
- Who or what motivates me?

Cautionary Reminder. Am I stuck?

Pentacles: The Realm of Grounding and Manifestation

Pentacles are about commitment, management, and embodiment. They move you from ideas to structure and from spark to steady progress. This is where you track your time, honor your body, manage your energy, and create tangible results. Pentacles invite you to plant your vision in the soil and tend it with patience.

Key Concepts. commitment, resources, structure, sustainability, embodiment, material world, fun, community, nature.

Over-Arching Question. Am I grounded in a clear, realistic plan?

Related Questions.
- What real-world steps will support this vision?
- What routines or tracking practices do I need to follow to stay on task?
- How can I build something that lasts?
- Whose help and guidance do I need?
- What budgets or material resources do I need to consider?
- What are the rewards that I will reap from this project?
- What social or relational capital can I count on?

- How can I work in a regenerative way and avoid draining resources?
- How can I listen to or gain support from Mother Earth or mirror nature's rhythms or cycles?

Cautionary Reminder. Do I lack a plan or support?

Weaving the Suits Together for Your Assistance

The Tarot framework can be a powerful tool for holistic thinking. Blending practical reflection with spiritual insight, Tarot helps you see the larger picture when your focus becomes caught in smaller details. Below are three practical ways the Minor Arcana suits can support the growth of your Vision Seed.

Initial Assessment. As you bring your Vision Seed to life, assess your project through the dimensions introduced in this chapter. Reflect on the questions under each Tarot suit to gain deeper insight into both your strengths and what might be missing. You may discover, for example, that you lack clarity or information about your Vision Seed under the lens of the Swords suit or that your Vision Seed feels misaligned with your Higher Purpose after examining it through the lens of the Cups. You might find that the Wands reveal a strong support system already in place, encouraging you to lean on your available resources.

Periodic Assessment. From time to time, revisit this framework as a way to check the "temperature" of your project. As in your initial assessment, ask yourself questions connected to each Tarot suit to identify blind spots and strengths. These reflections can reveal valuable insights and help you make meaningful adjustments, bringing your project to a greater level of clarity and impact.

Problem-Solving with Divination. Choose a traditional 78-card Tarot deck that includes both the Major and Minor Arcana. Remove the Major Arcana cards so that only the four suits—Swords, Cups, Wands, and Pentacles—remain. When you encounter a roadblock in your Vision Seed journey, draw one card at random and reflect on how its symbolism applies to your situation. For example, if you pull a Pentacles card, it may be a reminder to take a more grounded, practical approach. If you draw a Swords card, it may suggest a need for new knowledge or sharper insight. Trust that the Universe is guiding you toward the understanding you need at this time. You can also look up the specific meaning of the card you draw and consider how it relates to your current challenge. Refer to the keywords for each suit as points of reflection.

If you are comfortable interpreting the Major Archana cards, go for it. Use them to see what answers and insights they can provide for your project.

Visionary Practice: Exploring Frameworks

Frameworks greatly support project management. They help you see the complete picture, not just scattered tasks. They also support understanding, offering a structure that brings clarity to even the most complex ideas. Therefore, in this Visionary Practice, you are invited to create an alternative framework to hold all your codes so they no longer exist as a linear list but as an integrated, meaningful whole.

You will do this by shaping a visual map of your Higher Purpose Codex, using one defining word from each of your codes. These five words will serve as anchors, guiding you toward a deeper understanding of how your purpose, values, vision, Principles of Success, and Visionary Practices fit together.

Step One: Summarize. Return to each of your codes and summarize them into a single word. Let this word capture the core vibration or essence of the code. Do not overthink. Choose the word that feels alive, accurate, and emotionally true.

Step Two: Create Your Framework. Take a blank page and place your five words onto it in any structure that feels natural to you. You might choose:

- a mandala structure, placing one word at the center and the others around it
- a pyramid, arranging the codes with a key word on top and the rest placed in ascending levels of importance.
- a circle, a zigzag, or any pattern that feels aligned with your intuition

Let each placement carry intention. A word placed in the center can symbolize the code that nourishes or energizes all the others. A term positioned at the top of a pyramid may point to your highest guiding principle. When two words appear close together, their nearness can express the natural relationship they share within you. And if some words rest on the left side of your framework while others sit on the right, choose the significance behind that placement. The goal is to create a visual framework that helps you understand all of your codes better.

Step Three: Reflect and Integrate. When your framework feels complete, take a moment to look at what you have created. Notice what it reveals. Ask yourself: What energies sit at the heart of my journey? Then, gather your five words and complete the following sentence: *I am becoming someone who…*

Allow the sentence to unfold naturally. Let it be honest, spacious, and full of possibility. This powerful sentence, which integrates your different codes, can be almost like a second Higher Purpose Statement. Reflect on the possibilities and power of this new visual and textual addition to your codex.

Using the Research, Refine, Plan Strategy

TO TURN YOUR VISION SEED INTO A THRIVING REALITY, you need more than inspiration, you need a roadmap. One simple but powerful system for moving from idea to execution is the Research, Refine, and Plan (RRP) strategy, adapted from a method popularized by productivity expert and YouTuber Gillian Perkins. In her work, Perkins emphasizes the importance of breaking big goals into focused, practical steps.[1] Each stage builds momentum without overwhelm. This method is especially useful if you're juggling multiple ideas or feeling stuck about where to start. In this chapter, we'll explore how to apply each step to make your vision come to life.

Research: Turning Your Visionary Project into a Question

Research is a vital step toward manifestation. Whether your Vision Seed involves launching a business, conducting fieldwork, starting a healing practice, creating a community program, or deepening your spiritual life, it's essential to gather the knowledge that will help you walk forward with wisdom and clarity.

The Research stage reflects the Swords suit of the Tarot. It reflects the Swords because you're sharpening your questions. Knowledge acquisition traditionally begins with a question. When you ask powerful questions, you invite powerful answers. In this way, research becomes a sacred act of listening—to teachers, to educational materials, to communities, to the world, and to your own intuition.

Developing Research Questions

Before you gather resources, take time to articulate your central research question. This is the big, burning inquiry at the heart of your project. Once you name it, you can break it down into manageable sub-questions. For example, your central research question may be: *What do I need to understand to bring my community grief circles into reality?* This will lead you to further questions:

- What models already exist for community healing spaces?
- What do I need to host public gatherings?
- How can I make these circles culturally inclusive and trauma-informed?
- What is the cost of renting space, providing materials, and facilitating regularly?
- How do I center this work in my own ancestral traditions?

Developing a central research question can support any vision—whether you're starting a retreat center, launching a podcast, creating a spiritual mentorship program, or developing a local food garden.

Remember, you do not need to do your research alone. If you are struggling to think of answers to your central and sub-questions, consider using the following resources to find answers:

Mentorship and Conversations. Reach out to people who've walked a similar path. A single conversation can save you months of trial and error.

Books and Articles. Look for resources from experts, scholars, or practitioners in your field.

Online Courses or Trainings. Explore platforms like Coursera, Teachable, or YouTube to expand your skill-set.

Community Listening. If your vision serves a particular population, listen to their voices. Conduct surveys, hold listening sessions, or join online forums where they gather.

Spiritual Inquiry. Don't overlook non-academic forms of research like dreamwork, oracle readings, or meditation journeys. These too hold wisdom. Consider also connecting with Mother Earth, mountains, and other Biome Beings for answers to your questions.

While you may answer some of your sub-questions easily, other questions may take more time. It's possible, you might only answer your central question after completing your project.

Avoiding the Research Trap

While gaining knowledge is essential, beware of overdoing it. Some people get stuck in endless information-gathering because they're afraid to start. Let your research be purposeful and time-bound. You might set a research window: *I'll take two weeks to gather knowledge, make a few calls, and review three solid resources. Then I'll move into refinement.* Remember: research is not the project. It is the preparation for it.

As you gather insights, answers, and discoveries, it's important to create a dedicated space for your research to live. Whether it's a physical folder, a digital document, or a notebook set aside just for this purpose, let it become your Vision Seed research archive. This is where you'll store the gold you've uncovered—your questions, sub-questions, answers, resources, notes, inspirations, and early ideas.

Having all your findings in one place will make it easier to stay focused, refer to important information, and avoid starting over when distractions arise. Think of it as your project's home—a place you can return to for clarity, momentum, and direction whenever needed.

Refine: Choosing What Matters Most from Your Research

Once you've explored your ideas through research, the next phase is to Refine your vision into something actionable. This is where you take the wide landscape of your research and narrow your focus into something more defined and ultimately doable. Refining is like narrowing down your travel bucket list from ten destinations around the world to two or three that are close to one another because they align with your current budget and feel the most exciting or meaningful to visit right now. You're not abandoning your bigger dreams—you're simply choosing the ones that are most reachable and fulfilling at this stage.

In the Research stage, you may have encountered an array of directions your vision could take. You explored topics, found mentors, watched videos, followed leads, and filled pages with notes. The Refine stage now invites you to sift through all of that, and ask:

- What ideas feel the most aligned, promising, or exciting to pursue?
- Which direction feels most relevant right now?
- What's realistic to focus on in this season of my life?

An essential part of refining is learning to define your project's scope. Author Harold Kerzner (2022) explains project scope as drawing a clear boundary around what you are choosing to include and what you are not (at least for now). Think of it like packing a suitcase. You can't take everything with you, only what's most essential for your trip.

I learned the importance of defining the scope of a project while writing my dissertation. During my doctoral studies, I wrote a dissertation exploring the wisdom of both Yoga philosophy and Andean cosmology. In the beginning, I imagined including everything I'd ever learned—every concept and cultural nuance I could think of from both traditions. But once I began researching and compiling material, I quickly realized the scope was far too big. I was drowning in the topic's vastness. The Refine stage saved me.

I came to understand that the most powerful path forward wasn't in saying everything. Instead, I focused on a few things with clarity, depth, and resonance: five core teachings that both traditions held in common. That decision gave my project coherence and, most importantly, made it possible to finish. This is the power of refinement.

In-Scope vs Out-of-Scope

When you're clear about your scope, you're less likely to burn out or feel overwhelmed by trying to do everything at once.[2] The following exercise not only sharpens your focus, it conserves your energy.

Create a table with two columns to fill with what is in-scope and out-of-scope for you currently. In the "In-Scope" column, include the ideas, methods, or topics from your research that you feel ready and resourced to move forward with. These are the elements that you are seriously considering and that directly serve your Vision Seed. The items listed in the "In-Scope" column should align with your values and should be realistically actionable in the time frame and context you're working within.

In the "Out-of-Scope" column, include the ideas or inspirations that may be exciting or relevant, but are not part of your core focus right now. Take the items from your "Out-of-Scope" column and place them in a "parking lot" section of your journal or digital notes. You might return to this "parking lot" in the next season of your vision's unfolding or find they were seeds for something else entirely. Remember, placing an item in the "Out-of-Scope" column doesn't mean it's discarded. It simply means postponed.

Identifying Your Methods

Another way of refining your research is by defining the methods you will use to carry out your Vision Seed. In this context, methods are the intentional processes, tools, or routines you choose to turn your vision into reality. These methods reflect the Pentacles in the Tarot. They are part of the "how" behind your actions.

Community Work. If your Vision Seed is to support youth healing through storytelling, will you do this through workshops, a podcast, or one-on-one mentorship?

Coaching. If your Vision Seed is to build a wellness business, what model will you follow: group programs, private sessions, or a hybrid approach?

Writing. If your Vision Seed is to write a book, will you join a writer's circle, create character biographies and profiles, attend writing workshops, or block specific times for writing?

Identifying your methods allows you to refine your ideas in concrete ways.

SMART Goals

The SMART system is a well-known yet powerful goal-setting and planning structure. Use it to help you refine your Vision Seed.

S: Specific. What exactly are you trying to accomplish with your Vision Seed? Be precise. Instead of saying, *I want to share more about* *healing*, a more specific goal might be, *I want to launch a podcast series about ancestral healing practices.*

M: Measurable. How will you know you've succeeded? Ask yourself: How many? How much? What will change or be produced? For example, *I will release six episodes in two months*, or *I will teach three workshops this year.*

A: Achievable. Is this something I can realistically do, given my time, resources, and responsibilities? Avoid framing goals around things outside of your control (for example: *get a book deal*). Instead, rephrase them as*: Complete a manuscript and submit it to three publishers.* Identify obstacles early. Are there time, financial, or energy limitations? Make a plan to work with or around them.

R: Relevant. Do your methods and Vision Seed align with Higher Purpose? Ask: *Why do I want to do this? Is it meaningful to me? Is this the right time?* Sometimes, what we think we want is actually a placeholder for something deeper (for example: we want fame, when really, we need connection).

T: Time-Bound. Without a timeline, visions can stray. Set deadlines that are motivating but not rigid. For example, ask yourself: *What can I do in the next month? What can I do in the next three months? What can I do by the end of the year?*

Plan: Mapping Your Route and Celebrating Your Milestones

While having a clear end date brings urgency and structure to your goals, understanding how to get from where you are now to that finish line requires more than a deadline. It also requires a plan. The Plan stage is when you will identify the steps, resources, and timeline required to make steady progress and complete your project. In this way, the Plan stage reflects the Pentacles and Wands (action) in the Tarot.

You must identify your critical path to create an effective plan, which is the sequence of steps that must be completed, often in a specific order, to move your project forward.[3] For example, suppose your Vision Seed is to publish a book of poetry. Before you can publish, you must first finish the writing and editing. Before you can hire a cover designer, you'll need a title and concept. These dependencies form your critical path. Knowing what must come first (and what can wait) helps prevent overwhelm and wasted effort.

Building Your Plan

With clear steps and guiding markers, you'll be able to navigate the journey toward your Vision Seed one actionable decision at a time. Consider the following points when you are creating a plan for your project:

Start with Your End in Mind. What's the outcome you want to reach, and by when?

Work Backward From Your End Goal. List the big steps required to get there with target deadlines. These may be your milestones.

Identify Dependencies. Which steps rely on others being completed first? That's your critical path.

Leave Room for Flexibility in Your Plan. Do not plan rigidly. Life will happen. Stay open to adjusting as needed.

Prioritize the Most Important Tasks. What is time-sensitive? What must be done soon to keep your momentum alive? Organize your plan around important dates. Some questions that can be helpful are: What can wait? What needs to be completed altogether?

Along your critical path, it's equally important to define your milestones: key markers that show you are making meaningful progress. Milestones are measurable, achievable events that confirm momentum and offer opportunities for reflection, course correction, and celebration. For example, if your Vision Seed is to publish a collection of short stories, your milestones might look like:

- finish writing twenty short stories
- choose the top ten
- hire an editor
- design the book layout
- submit to a small press or self-publish

These milestones help you celebrate progress while keeping your end goal in sight. Ideally, you'll identify 3–5 major milestones that will guide the phases of your project. Plan what your celebration may look like. Are you opening a bottle of champagne or going out to your favorite restaurant? Don't hold back. Make celebration of milestones an important ritual in your journey.

Project Dashboards: What Gets Monitored, Gets Done

THERE IS AN EASY WAY TO KNOW if your vehicle is functioning properly. You simply glance down and check the car's dashboard. The gas gauge informs if you have enough fuel for the trip. You check the speedometer to see whether you are going too fast or falling behind. The temperature settings help control comfort and airflow in the vehicle. Some dashboards even include a GPS system, showing exactly where you are on the map, how far you've come, and what turn to make next.

In the world of business strategy, "dashboards" have become an essential tool. One expert in project management is Harold Kerzner, Sr. Executive Director for Project Management at The International Institute for Learning. In his book, *Project Management Metrics, KPIs, and Dashboard: A Guide to Measuring and Monitoring Project Performance* (2022), he describes dashboards as compact visual tools that help individuals monitor key performance indicators (KPIs) and take meaningful action based on real-time insights. In short, dashboards help you monitor your progress and make decisions.

The same level of insight and simplicity can apply to your personal goals. Just like a car dashboard shows you how your vehicle is operating, a personal project dashboard shows you how your project is operating. It helps you monitor your progress. Without one, it's easy to get lost in the details, lose track of what matters most, or miss early signs that something is veering off course. Your dashboard doesn't have to be high-tech or complicated; it just needs to be meaningful to you. Whether your dashboard resembles a car, a garden, or a musical orchestra, it can become a powerful ally in keeping your purpose alive and on track. In this chapter, we'll explore how to create a personal project dashboard that reflects your unique goals and metaphorical style.

What Your Dashboard Needs to Monitor

The heart of project monitoring is deciding what truly matters. Before you build a dashboard, or even choose a metaphor for it, you first need to get clear on what aspects of your Vision Seed you need to monitor. A dashboard only becomes useful when it reflects the right signals—those vital indicators that let you know if your project is healthy, aligned, and moving forward. This means not every detail of your work belongs on the dashboard. In fact, a cluttered dashboard could do more harm than good. The goal is to surface the key indicators that deserve your regular attention, so you can respond wisely when they shift out of range. To figure out what needs to be on your dashboard, ask yourself:

- *What signals tell me I'm on track with my Vision Seed?*
- *What signs alert me when I'm drifting,*
  stalling, or burning out?
- *What elements of my project need regular care, evaluation, or*
  balancing?

The answers to these questions will be what Kerzner (2022) refers to as Key Performance Indicators (KPIs): the specific, measurable conditions that reflect progress toward a goal. These are your priority indicators that you need to monitor—the equivalents of fuel, speed, temperature, and direction on a car's dashboard. They may include:

- **tasks:** key tasks that lead you to achieve your milestones
- **energy**: key places where you need to focus your energy
- **resources**: key tools, funds, or materials that need to be replenished
- **alignment**: key insights connected to your Higher Purpose
- **well-being**: key life areas where you need to maintain health, rest, or flourishing relationships

You might also want to track less tangible but equally meaningful signals like how many courageous or uncomfortable steps you've taken this week or whether you're meeting resistance that signals growth rather than burnout. Your KPIs may not be about profit margins or client leads in a business sense. Instead, they might be about other measures of success related to your energy, balance, integrity, or creative momentum. What matters is that they are relevant to your project and actionable in real life.

A dashboard doesn't just serve you at the beginning of your Vision Seed process. It can serve you at any stage. Whether you're still in the early phases of building something new or in the ongoing rhythm of maintaining what you've created, a dashboard offers insight and guidance. For instance, if your Vision Seed is to open a restaurant, your pre-launch dashboard might monitor tasks like finding a location, finalizing the menu, and decorating the space. Once the restaurant is open, your operational dashboard might track daily revenue, staff morale, or guest satisfaction. Different phases require different KPIs, but both phases benefit from intentional tracking.

Choosing a Metaphor for Your Dashboard

After you decide what truly needs to be monitored, the next step is choosing a dashboard metaphor that fits the nature of your Vision

Seed. While a personalized metaphor is optional, it is highly recommended. A well-chosen metaphor is not decorative; it shapes how you relate to your project. When the metaphor fits, the dashboard comes to life and becomes a tool that feels meaningful.

Your metaphor can directly reflect the nature of your project. For example, if your Vision Seed is related to music, your dashboard might resemble a recording studio. Your "gauges" could include the live room, vocal booth, control room, or lounge area—each representing different aspects of creative output, such as collaboration, practice, focus, or rest.

If your Vision Seed involves personal transformation, such as rebuilding life after a major transition, your dashboard might resemble a weather report. In this case, you may track mood patterns, energy levels, support systems, and moments of courage. Storms, seasons, and recovery periods become meaningful signals, helping you respond with compassion rather than judgment.

Your metaphor does not need to be directly related to your project. For instance, you might use the metaphor of a long road trip. Here, destinations represent milestones, marking meaningful progress along the way. The roads between destinations reflect tasks—some smooth and fast, others slow or demanding. Planned arrival times function as a schedule "gauge," helping you monitor pacing. Fuel levels or engine temperature signal when rest, support, or maintenance is needed. Weather and road conditions reflect external constraints such as delays, detours, or circumstances beyond your control. What matters most is not the metaphor itself, but that your dashboard makes sense and helps you notice what needs attention.

How to Track Key Performance Indicators (KPIs)

After you identify a metaphor and what your dashboard needs to monitor, choose how you'll track signals. Ask yourself what symbols or check-in tools will help you stay aware without feeling overwhelmed. In his book, Kerzner (2022) outlines several types of visual components used in business dashboards. While originally created for executives and organizations, these tools can be meaningfully adapted to personal and visionary projects. The point isn't to be flashy; it's being clear. Think of these components as providing you with alerts that you can respond to.

Below are a few simple types of indicators you can use in your project dashboard. You don't have to use all of these. In fact, simplicity is key. Choose one or two visual styles that resonate with you and reflect the nature of what you're tracking. Remember, these tools are not here to police you; they are here to support you in navigating real life, with all its complexity.

Traffic Light Icons. Green, Yellow, Red. These basic color indicators help you quickly assess the current state of a key area:

> green = all is well
> yellow = pay attention
> red = immediate action needed

You can use these colors or traffic light icons for daily, weekly, or monthly check-ins, giving each area a quick status rating. For example: energy level (green), progress on writing (yellow), alignment with purpose (green), or finance (red).

Trend Arrows. Trend arrows track whether something is improving, declining, or holding steady.

> ↑ = getting better
> ↓ = getting worse
> → = holding steady

You can apply these to internal measures like motivation or outward ones like outreach efforts or income.

Percentage Completion. Sometimes the best way to track progress is simply by estimating how far along you are toward a milestone in percentage form. This doesn't require an app or automation, just your honest assessment. You can assign a percentage to any measurable task or phase of your project. For example:

business plan = ■■■■■■□□□ 70% complete
outreach emails = ■■■■□□□□□ 40% sent
website = ■■■■■■■□ 90% complete

This kind of tracking is especially helpful during extensive projects, when it's easy to feel stuck or unsure of how much you've really accomplished. Seeing that you're 60% done can offer a boost of motivation. It reminds your brain that movement is happening, even if the finish line isn't quite in sight yet. You can jot down your completion percentages weekly or monthly in a journal, planner, or notebook. The goal isn't to be mathematically perfect. It's staying connected to the feeling of forward motion.

My Fieldwork Dashboard

During my doctoral fieldwork in Peru, my research involved both academic study and deep spiritual engagement. It included facilitating pilgrimage experiences, surveying retreat participants, and completing an immersive apprenticeship with spiritual elders. The work required careful attention not only to logistics and research protocols but also to my own inner alignment and the subtle emergence of sacred knowledge.

To stay grounded and on track in my project, I designed a weekly dashboard to monitor the most important elements of my research, using a yogic metaphor I described in an earlier chapter of this book: "The Chariot and the Charioteer." My dashboard contained a story that kept me grounded and inspired.

The Charioteer. I was the charioteer—the one holding the reins, making directional decisions, and striving to remain centered.

The Reins. Although the reins were not included in the visual of the dashboard, they symbolized my discernment—my capacity to guide wisely, moment by moment, based on both observation and intuition. I imagined them around the four horses I was monitoring.

The Four Horses. Each horse represented a critical "gauge" or aspect of the project that needed weekly monitoring and care. The horses represented:

1. **research execution**: Were fieldwork activities (pilgrimages, camps, interviews) unfolding in alignment with the plan?
2. **spiritual practice**: Was I maintaining a strong connection with my practices, teachers, and ceremonies?
3. **data gathering**: Was I consistently collecting and organizing my research materials— surveys, memos, recordings?
4. **emergent knowledge**: Was I capturing the new insights, themes, and teachings that surfaced through experience?

Progress Indicators. A right pointing arrow, caution sign, X, and a star offered a quick visual check-in for how each horse was "running the course".

 on track and thriving

⚠ needs attention or clarity

✗ off track or struggling

☆ favorable outcome, spontaneous breakthrough

Charioteer Assessment. Inside the dashboard, I created a space (supportive analytics) for me to write brief notes reflecting on where I felt clear and where I sensed I needed to adjust.

Figure 3

"Chariot and the Charioteer" Project Dashboard

	May 5-11	May 12-18	May 19-25
Horse 1: Research Execution	⚠	☆	☆
Horse 2: Spiritual Practice	→	☆	→
Horse 3: Data Gathering	✗	⚠	⚠
Horse 4: Emergent Knowledge	⚠	⚠	⚠
Charioteer Assessment (Supportive Analytics)	*This week I am delayed in deploying the consent forms.*	*Kinship camp began as planned, but I am still missing two consent forms.*	*Kinship Camp complete. Some participants still have not signed the consent form.*

This dashboard helped me hold both the structure and the spirit of my research. When arrows changed to Xs, I knew to pause and investigate. Each week, my dashboard answered whether I was falling behind on data entry. *Was burnout creeping in? Was insight emerging that I hadn't yet recorded?*

What I learned is that a personal dashboard doesn't just help you stay on task. It helps you stay in relationship with your project, your values, and yourself. It becomes a motivator too. Whenever my project reached an important milestone or something new and valuable emerged, I enjoyed marking it with a star. These small motivators can really enhance your journey and make big projects more enjoyable. Whether you're preparing to launch a vision or sustaining one already in motion, your dashboard becomes a reflection of your awareness and care. Figure 3 is an example of the table I used to monitor my dashboard.

Supportive Analytics: Reconnecting with Your "Why." As I worked with my "Chariot and the Charioteer" dashboard week by week, I began to notice something important: while the symbols helped me see what was happening in each area of my project, they didn't always explain why things were shifting. A "needs attention" symbol on "research execution" one week might signal a delay or it might be pointing to a deeper disconnection or fatigue. That's why you will need more than visual indicators. You need a space for reflection—a way to track the patterns behind the patterns.

This is what Kerzner (2011) refers to as supportive analytics, the context and insights that sit beneath the surface of your indicators. In business, this might look like tracing a dip in sales back to a marketing gap or new competition. In personal projects, it can be more subtle. It helps you make sense of what your dashboard is trying to tell you.

Supporting analytics invites you into a deeper dialogue with your process. When something on your dashboard slips from green to yellow or yellow to red, you get curious. If a project goes from a green flag to yellow, you may ask: *is it due to lack of time, emotional heaviness, or avoidance of something deeper?* If you see an indicator that the project has stalled, you may think*: am I unclear about my next step? Am I confident about my direction? Am I simply in need of rest?* If you feel misaligned, you may take it as a signal to refine your plan or a call to reconnect with your "why." Through this kind of inquiry and reflection, you start to gather the kind of information need to make wise, compassionate adjustments.

Supportive analytics processing can be done in many forms:

- weekly reflection notes that ask what worked and what didn't
- a check-in journal where you track sleep, mood, energy, or focus
- short voice memos capturing insights or challenges
- conversations with trusted mentors or peers
- observations about your environment or stress patterns

Remember, your dashboard can live in an app or a spreadsheet. You can draw it in your journal or sketch it on a whiteboard. The location doesn't matter. What matters is that it's usable, helpful and yours. Whatever form and metaphor you choose, remember the main objective is to create enough awareness that your dashboard becomes not just a measurement tool but also a mirror.

Watching Your Seed Bloom with a Visionary Action Plan

FROM THE TAROT SUITS as a framework for balancing the many dimensions of your project to the RRP strategy that walks you through a research process, you've explored what it takes to bring your vision to life. Further, you've learned how to define what's in-scope and what's not, how to follow your critical path, and how to set milestones that affirm your progress along the way. You learned to create a project dashboard, a personal system for staying in tune with your process. These tools are here to support one thing: your becoming.

Visionary Practice: Watching Your Seed Bloom with a Visionary Action Plan

Step One: Brainstorming. Make a list of three to five project management tools to help you structure the growth and progress of your Vision Seed.

Step Two: Revisit the Higher Purpose Codex. Then, write your sixth code.

Code Six
To grow my Vision Seed with clarity and direction,
I will create the following Visionary Action Plan...

Sample
To provide clarity and direction for my Vision Seed, I will create the following Visionary Action Plan: use the Tarot suits as a lens for project analysis, identify what is in-scope or out-of-scope when creating the critical path, create SMART goals for planning, and employ a project dashboard to help monitor my progress.

Step Three: Reflecting. Write about each project management tool you chose, and describe why they are important to you. Write what feels resonant now, knowing you can update this list as your Vision Seed develops.

MILESTONE MARKER. Excellent work! You made it all the way to writing the sixth code in your Higher Purpose Codex. Thank you for being here and for all the good the world will receive from your hard work. It is truly an honor for me to work with you. I consider us fellow pilgrims on life's journey of discovery. Please reach out to share your accomplishments with me and don't forget to celebrate later all the things you achieved.

Final Weavings and Invitations

THERE'S AN OLD SAYING ABOUT TWO PEOPLE LAYING BRICKS. When asked what they are doing, the first replies, "I'm laying bricks." The second, asked the same question, answers with a visionary outlook: "I'm building a cathedral."

No one knows where this story comes from, but its wisdom has lasted because it reveals something essential. When you look beneath the surface of what you are doing and uncover the need behind the want—the why beneath the action—you begin to understand the powerful role purpose plays in your life. Sometimes, it can transform something as basic as stacking bricks into something sacred.

At times, your Vision Seed will have tedious tasks and a number of obstacles that will make you want to lose your mind. When this happens, return to your Higher Purpose, revisit your Principles of Success, and adopt what author and psychologist Carol S. Dweck calls a growth mindset. Naming your Vision Seed and clearly imagining the final outcome does not mean it will immediately take physical form, nor does it exempt you from hard work.

This is where trust is required. Can you trust the old saying, "'Becoming is better than being?'"[1] Becoming invites movement, humility, and growth. Don't waste your time needing to be flawless or perfect. It will only slow you down. Instead embrace your becoming. Enjoy the journey—with all of its obstacles. Meet each challenge with steady effort and firm determination, knowing that every step you take—especially the difficult ones—is carrying you closer to your goal.

Here is a final reminder to take all the codes you have written in this book and weave them together making any necessary adjustments that feel true at this time:

Higher Purpose Codex

Code One
My Higher Purpose is...

Code Two
My Core Values for interacting with others are...
My Core Values for keeping peace with myself are...

Code Three
To bring my Higher Purpose to action, I will
plant the following Vision Seed(s)...

Code Four
To help my Vision Seed take root and thrive,
these are my Principles of Success...

Code Five
To ensure my mental and spiritual expansion, I will
engage with the following Visionary Practices...

Code Six
To provide clarity and direction for my Vision Seed, I
will create the following Visionary Action Plan...

The Personal Map of Your Becoming

Your Higher Purpose Codex doesn't need to be a single list or a scroll of poetic affirmations, unless you want it to be. This is your personal map of becoming, and you're free to design it in a way that feels expansive and meaningful. Be creative and consider structuring your codex in a circular way or in a way that aligns with your cultural background.

Besides writing your codes, consider creating a binder, folder, or journal with six labeled sections or pockets, one for each of the codex entries. Here, you can archive supplementary notes for each of your codes. In your Visionary Practices folder, for example, you might include:

- instructions for meditations or rituals
- a copy of your astrological chart and notes from your own reflections
- journal entries or drawings inspired by dreamwork or oracular guidance
- teachings from a spiritual mentor or tradition you're following

Let your codex evolve, and create a library of tools to support each one of them. You might include reminders of sacred moments or collect quotes that mirror your intentions. Whether it lives in a digital folder, a beautiful leather binder, or a collage-covered notebook, let it be a sacred companion that reminds you of who you truly are.

As Your Vision Seed Blooms...

Bringing a Vision Seed to bloom involves lots of hard work, as well as faith in your intuition. It asks you to engage with your purpose not just as a dreamer, but as a gardener—someone willing to water and nurture the seed that wants to grow through you. Remember, your

Vision Seed is both a gift in your life and a gift you are offering to the world. When you give your care, your clarity, and your consistent attention, your Vision Seed can take root in ways you may not yet imagine.

As your guide, I offer you one final encouragement: trust that through the teachings of this book, you have built the inner foundation needed to feel more respect, connection, and belonging with the outer world. These are vital for every human being. In fact, in a future book, we may do a deep dive into the code of belonging. Until then, trust that you are ready to enjoy all that life offers, including the esteem and acceptance of your peers, as you seek to live in harmony with the world around you.

It is an honor for me that you have come all this way, though not just because I honor your dedication. I honor your ancestors walking beside you. They cheer you on. They live through you. I honor the Divine within you. Thank you for letting me connect with you, and your inner network of ancestors and guides, in the glorious unfolding of your journey.

References

Invitation: Find the Ruby in Your Heart

1. *Viktor Emil Frankl.* (n.d.). Viktor Frankl Institute. https://www.viktor-frankl.org/biography.html
2. Sarkar, S. P. R. (1959). *Idea and ideology.* Ananda Marga Publications.

What Being Human Reveals About Your Purpose

1. Anandamurti, S. S. (2009). Where there is Dharma there is *iśta*, and where there is *iśta* there is victory. *Subhāśita Samgraha* Part 12. Electronic Edition. Ánanda Márga Pracáraka Samgha.
2. Shaffer, J., Johnson, E., & Frederickson, B. (2016). Neuroplasticity and clinical practice: Building brain power for health. *Frontiers in Psychology,* 7, 1118. https://www.frontiersin.org/journals/psychology/articles/10.3389/fpsyg.2016.01118/full
3. Alexander, S., & Baraz, J. (2010, February). The helper's high. *Greater Good Magazine.* https://greatergood.berkeley.edu/article/item/the_helpers_high
4. Filkowski, M., Cochran, R. N., & Haas, B. (2016). Altruistic behavior: mapping responses in the brain. *Neuroscience and Neuroeconomics,* Volume 5, 65–75. https://www.dovepress.com/altruistic-behavior-mapping-responses-in-the-brain-peer-reviewed-fulltext-article-NAN
5. *Empathy and oxytocin lead to greater generosity.* (2007, November 7). Science Daily. https://www.sciencedaily.com/releases/2007/11/071107074321.htm
6. United Nations. (n.d.). *Honouring Rabindranath Tagore.* UnitedNations. https://www.un.org/en/academic-impact/honouring-rabindranath-tagore

Sources referenced without a subscript:

- Anandamurti, S. S. (1957). *Guide to human conduct*. Ananda Marga Publications.
- Dweck, C. S. (2006). *Mindset: The new psychology of success*. Ballantine Books.

Weaving Together Code One: Revealing Who You Really Are

1. Alshami A. M. (2019). Pain: Is It All in the Brain or the Heart?. *Current Pain and Headache Reports*, *23*(12), 88.

Invitation: "Don't Be Evil"

1. Cuthbertson, A. (2018, May 21). Google quietly removes 'don't be evil' preface from code of conduct | The Independent. *The Independent*. https://www.the-independent.com/tech/google-dont-be-evil-code-conduct-removed-alphabet-a8361276.html

Truth with Kindness: The Practice of Satya

1. Anandamurti, S. S. (1957). *Guide to human conduct*. Ananda Marga Publications. Ananda Marga Publications.

Building a World Without Theft: The Wisdom of Asteya

1. Chen, H., & Magramo, K. (2024, February 4). Finance worker pays out $25 million after video call with deepfake 'chief financial officer.' CNN. https://www.cnn.com/2024/02/04/asia/deepfake-cfo-scam-hong-kong-intl-hnk
2. Farrow, R. (2022, April 18). How democracies spy on their citizens. *The New Yorker*. https://www.newyorker.com/magazine/2022/04/25/how-democracies-spy-on-their-citizens

The True Meaning of *Brahmacharya*

1. Anandamurti, S. S. (1957). *Guide to human conduct*. Ananda Marga Publications.

The End of Excess: Practicing *Aparigraha*

1. Balch, O. (2013, February 18). The relevance of Gandhi in the capitalism debate. *The Guardian*. https://www.theguardian.com/sustainable-business/blog/relevance-gandhi-capitalism-debate-rajni-bakshi

Clean Body, Clear Mind: Living with Shaocha

1–2. Sarkar, P. R. (1981). *The liberation of intellect: Neohumanism.* Ananda Marga Publications.

More Than Kindness: Understanding Tapah

1. Jacobs, H. A. (2000). *Incidents in the life of a slave girl: Written by herself.* Penguin Books.

When Scripture Heals, and When it Harms: The Need for *Svadhyaya*

1. Sobieski, M. A. (2025, April 7). Scripture as a weapon: How the Confederacy's biblical justification of oppression still echoes today | Milwaukee Independent. *Milwaukee Independent.* https://www.milwaukeeindependent.com/column/scripture-weapon-confederacys-biblical-justification-oppression-still-echoes-today/

2–4. *English standard version Bible.* (2001). Crossway Bibles.

Accelerating the Soul's Journey: The Practice of Iishvara Pranidhana

Anandamurti, S. S. (1982). "An Introduction to Shiva (Discourse 1)." *Namah shivaya shantaya.* Ananda Marga Publications. Print.

2. Sarkar, S. P. R. (1959). Pratisaincara and manah. *Idea and ideology.* Ananda Marga Publications.

Invitation: Trace Your Vision Back to Its Roots

1–3. Conteh, K. (2024). *How my brother's death inspired my journey into healthcare.* [Unpublished student paper]. Department of Languages and Social Sciences, Northern Virginia Community College.

4. British and Foreign Bible Society. (n.d.). Ecclesiastes 3 (KJV). Bible Society. https://www.biblesociety.org.uk/explore-the-bible/read/eng/KJV/Eccl/3/

Invitation: Learn the "Seven" Secrets of Success

1, 3. Bjonnes, R. (2018). *A brief history of yoga: From its Tantric roots to the modern yoga studio.* Inner World Publications.

2. Anandamurti. (1967). *Ánanda vacanámrtam* Part 23. Ananda Marga Publications.

Firm Determination: Bridging Skill and Achievement

1. Duckworth, A. (2016). *Grit: The power of passion and perseverance.* Scribner.

2. Farnsworth, H. (2023, October 3). *Helpful hints from Psych Department professors! They know a thing or two…* Roanoke College Psychology Department. https://psych.pages.roanoke.edu/2023/10/03/helpful-hints-from-psych-department-professors-they-know-a-thing-or-two/

3. Gladwell, M. (2011). *Outliers: The story of success.* Back Bay Books.

4. Ananadamurti. (1978). *Subháśita samgraha.* Part 11. Ananda Marga Publications.

5. Ananadamurti. (1958). *Subháśita samgraha.* Part 7. Ananda Marga Publications.

6. Traugott, J. (2014, August 26). *Achieving your goals: An evidence-based approach.* MSU Extension. https://www.canr.msu.edu/news/achieving_your_goals_an_evidence_based_approach

Pursuing Universal Truth: Trading Glitter for Gold

1, 5, 7. Hari, J. (2018). *Lost connections: Uncovering the real causes of depression—and the unexpected solutions.* Bloomsbury Publishing.

2–4. Hari, J. (2018, January 21). We know junk food makes us sick. Are "junk values" making us depressed? *Los Angeles Times.* https://www.latimes.com/opinion/op-ed/la-oe-hari-kasser-junk-values-20180121-story.html

6. Simpson, J. (2022, April 14). Finding brand success in the digital world. *Forbes.* https://www.forbes.com/sites/forbesagencycouncil/2017/08/25/finding-brand-success-in-the-digital-world/

8. Evans, J., Lesage, K., Miner, W., Starr, K. J., & Corichi, M. (2025, May 6). God, spirits and the natural world. Pew Research Center. https://www.pewresearch.org/religion/2025/05/06/god-spirits-and-the-natural-world/

Finding the Right Guide: Choosing Teachers Who Uplift

1. Hecker, H. (2007). Angulimala: A murderer's road to sainthood. Access to Insight. https://www.accesstoinsight.org/lib/authors/hecker/wheel312.html

2. Vedaprajinananda, D. (2016). *Wisdom of Tantra: An Introduction to Ananda Marga Philosophy* (2nd ed.). Innerworld Publications.

3. Anandamurti, S. S. (2009). Some Characters of the Mahábhárata. *Discourses on the Mahabharata.* Electronic Edition. Ánanda Márga Pracáraka Samgha.

Sources referenced without a subscript:

• Clear, J. (2018). *Atomic habits.* Random House Business Books.

Steadiness of Mind: Balance, Breath and Belonging

1. Vedaprajinananda, D. (2016). *Wisdom of Tantra: An Introduction to Ananda Marga Philosophy* (2nd ed.). Innerworld Publications.
2. Docter, P., & Del Carmen, R. (Directors). (2015). *Inside out* [Film]. Walt Disney Pictures; Pixar Animation Studios.
3–4. Guy-Evans, O. G. (2025, May 22). Sympathetic Nervous System: Functions & examples. *Simply Psychology.* https://www.simplypsychology.org/sympathetic-nervous-system.html
5. Vishvarupananda, D., personal communication, (May 28, 2017).
6. Chopra, D. (2020). *Total meditation: Practices in living the awakened life.* Harmony Books.
7–8. TEDx Talks. (2018, November 29). *How to build self confidence | CeCe Olisa | TEDxFresnoState* [Video]. YouTube. https://www.youtube.com/watch?v=ivNNgdCsY7o
9. Tajfel, H., Billig, M., Bundy, R. P., & Flament, C. (1971). "Social categorization and intergroup behaviour." *European Journal of Social Psychology,* 1, 149–178.
10. Dweck, C. S. (2006). *Mindset: The new psychology of success.* Ballantine Books.

Sources referenced without a subscript:

- Brown, B. (2012). *Daring greatly: How the courage to be vulnerable transforms the way we live, love, parent, and lead.* Avery.

Embracing Self-Restraint: Moving Beyond Impulse

1. Vishvarupananda, D., personal communication, (May 28, 2017).
2–3. Hadad, C. (2015, July 10). *What the "Marshmallow Test" can teach you about your kids.* CNN. https://www.cnn.com/2014/12/22/us/marshmallow-test/index.html
4–5. Arablouei, R. (Host). (2019, August 22). *Strange fruit* [Audio podcast transcript]. In Throughline NPR. https://www.npr.org/transcripts/752909807

Sources referenced without a subscript:

- Hari, J. (2016). *Chasing the scream: The first and last days of the war on drugs.* Bloomsbury Publishing.

Caring for the Body: Fuel, Movement, and Reverence

1. Esquivel M. K. (2022). Nutrition benefits and considerations for whole

foods plant-based eating patterns. *American Journal of Lifestyle Medicine, 16*(3), 284–290.

2–3. TEDx Talks. (2016, July 20). *What is the best diet for humans? | Eran Segal | TEDxRuppin* [Video]. Youtube. https://www.youtube.com/watch?v=0z03xkwFbw4

4. Collins, T., and Luger, C. (2022). *The seven circles: Indigenous teachings for living well.* Harper Collins.

5. Sissons, B. (2025, July 2). *What is functional strength training, and how can I get started?* Medical News Today. https://www.medicalnewstoday.com/articles/functional-strength-training

6–7. Vishvarupananda, D., personal communication, (May 7, 2017).

Sources referenced without a subscript:

• Pollan, M. (2007). *The omnivore's dilemma: A natural history of four meals.* Penguin.

Weaving Together Code Four: Declaring Your Principles of Success

1–2. Anandamurti, S. S. (1978). The seven secrets of success. *Ánanda vacanámrtam*, Part 3. Ananda Marga Publications.

Invitation: Become a Visionary Practitioner

1–2. Winfrey, O. (2012, February). *What Oprah knows for sure about finding the fullest expression of yourself.* Oprah. https://www.oprah.com/health/oprah-on-stillness-and-meditation-oprah-visits-fairfield-iowa

3. Bowen, D. (2018, November 20). Gloria Anzaldúa: From Borderlands to Nepantla. *Oxford Research Encyclopedia of Communication.* Retrieved 17 Sep. 2025, from https://oxfordre.com/communication/view/10.1093/acrefore/9780190228613.001.0001/acrefore-9780190228613-e-606

4. Baer, D. (2015, January 9). Here's how Zen meditation changed Steve Jobs' life and sparked a design revolution. *Business Insider.* https://www.businessinsider.com/steve-jobs-zen-meditation-buddhism-2015-1

5. Shontell, A. (2013, September 11). The last gift Steve Jobs gave to family and friends was a book about self realization. *Business Insider.* https://www.businessinsider.com/steve-jobs-gave-yoganandas-book-as-a-gift-at-his-memorial-2013-9

Visionary Practice: Going on Sacred Journeys

Kuntur, T. & Kuntur, I.T. (2019). *Tukuy t'ikray: The path of conscious transformation for the cosmic being.* Escuela Solar Inka.

Visionary Practice: Asserting Your Archetypal Identity

1. A. Filemyr, personal communication, (January 22, 2025).
2. Columbia Law School. (2017, June 8). *Kimberlé Crenshaw on intersectionality, more than two decades later.* Columbia Law School. https://www.law.columbia.edu/news/archive/kimberle-crenshaw-intersectionality-more-two-decades-later

Visionary Practice: Developing Kinship with an Animal or Biome Guide

1. Peacock, T., & Wisuri, M. (2002). *Ojibwe waasa inaabidaa: We look in all directions.* Minnesota Historical Society Press.

Invitation: Map the Path Ahead with Visionary Tools

1. Pollack, R. (2019). *Seventy-eight degrees of wisdom: A tarot journey to self-awareness* (2nd ed.). Weiser Books.

Using the Research, Refine, Plan Strategy

1. Gillian, P. (2020, September 8). *How to set goals & create an action plan! (Step-by-step tutorial)* [Video]. YouTube. https://www.youtube.com/watch?v=jf7FUSH9pVk
2–3. Lock, D. (2016). *The essentials of project management* (4th ed.). Routledge.

Sources referenced without a subscript:

• Kerzner, H. (2022). *Project management metrics, KPIs, and dashboards: A guide to measuring and monitoring project performance* (4th ed.). Wiley.

Project Dashboards: Seeing Your Progress Clearly

Sources referenced without a subscript:

• Kerzner, H. (2022). *Project management metrics, KPIs, and dashboards: A guide to measuring and monitoring project performance* (4th ed.). Wiley.

Final Weavings and Invitations

1. Dweck, C. S. (2006). *Mindset: The new psychology of success.* Ballantine Books.

Those Who Made the Path Possible

My deepest gratitude (*añay*) goes first to *Pachamama*, the Cosmic Mother, and *Pachatayta*, the Cosmic Father. For the Universe itself had to be conceived and sustained for any of the following to happen.

Many of the people named here I have known for more than twenty years. My gratitude for them extends far beyond their contributions to this book. They have shaped my life, my values, and my becoming in ways that words can only partially tell.

Thank you David for coming with me on my first meditation retreat when you were only ten years old, even though I did not have Mom's permission to drive you out to the retreat in Missouri. Dada V, Dada Gana, and the entire Ananda Marga community, thank you for giving me a spiritual home. A timeless thank you goes to Shrii Shrii Anandamurti (*Baba*), whose legacy I humbly strive to carry forward.

Thank you to Dr. Ann Filemyr and the Southwestern College community for inviting students and seekers to plant Vision Seeds and grow into regenerative leaders, and to Gustavo Prudente, for teaching me how to coach and guide people in remembering their Higher Purpose.

Thank you to my nest—Andra, Matiss, and Aviana—and to the rest of my family. Andra, your beautiful designs and extraordinary gifts bring beauty, coherence, and meaning to everything we create together.

Thank you to Laura June Rose for content editing, and to David Epstein, Stephanie Harm, and all my colleagues at Northern Virginia Community College for trusting me to share these teachings within our college community.

Gratitude also goes to my Quechua *ayllu* (community) in the Andes, to Tupac T'ito Kuntur and to the ancestors, biome beings, and more-than-human kin whom I look to for guidance and answers.

Finally, enormous gratitude goes to my readers, students, and spiritual friends. Together, and with everyone mentioned here, we are on a mission guided by *llankay* (effort), *munay* (love), and *yachay* (wisdom) to offer a beautiful vision back to this sacred planet.

Añay. Añay. Añay.

GUSTAVO MONJE is a professor of College Writing and Literature at Northern Virginia Community College, where he has taught since 2006. Drawing from many years of teaching purpose-building principles to his students, his book, *Stuck in Yesterday* will be available as a textbook starting in Spring, 2026. Recognized by his native Quechua lineage as a *Yachacha Pampa Paqo* (Shaman of Wisdom), he integrates Andean spirituality with yogic traditions, leading treks and healing journeys in Peru. Monje coaches individuals and groups in purpose building, meditation, and other Indigenous wellness practices. He is the creator of @GustavoMonjePhD, a Youtube channel with over 20,000 subscribers, and holds a yoga alliance certificate in Tantra Yoga. He is currently a PhD candidate in Visionary Practice and Regenerative Leadership at Southwestern College and the New Earth Institute. Work with Gustavo Monje and join his community by visiting:

www.gustavomonje.com

youtube.com/@GustavoMonjePhD

facebook.com/GustavoMonjePhD

instagram.com/GustavoMonjePhD

www.ingramcontent.com/pod-product-compliance
Lightning Source LLC
Chambersburg PA
CBHW021219130626
46554CB00004B/1273